Crosscurrents / MODERN CRITIQUES

Harry T. Moore, *General Editor*

NATHANAEL WEST'S
Novels

Irving Malin

WITH A PREFACE BY

Harry T. Moore

SOUTHERN ILLINOIS UNIVERSITY PRESS
Carbondale and Edwardsville

FEFFER & SIMONS, INC.
London and Amsterdam

Contents

Preface

Irving Malin, a City College professor who has written several earlier books for the Crosscurrents/Modern Critiques series, gives us in the present volume a thorough and expert view of the novels of Nathanael West.

Somewhat of a New Critic in his approach, Dr. Malin asserts that textual analysis is the most important element in discussions of a writer's work, and of course he is right in this. He doesn't, however, altogether dismiss the value of social and biographical considerations, though in his examinations of West's four novels he sticks closely to the texts.

But a bit of Nathanael West biography won't hurt anyone. Even in this book with its New Critics' idea of concentrating on the texts, the author can't help making a few comments on West's background. So, here are a few facts which may help to place this novelist in his milieu.

West, born in 1903, was named Nathan Wallenstein Weinstein, the name he used in his Brown University days. After some academic difficulties at Tufts, he had gone to Brown on the strength of Nathan Weinstein's transcript. This was the record of another Nathan Weinstein—just the zany kind of event which might occur at any moment in West's fiction. Despite the fakery, he was graduated from Brown in 1924 and then went to Europe for a couple of years spent mostly in Paris. After his return he became assistant manager at two uptown New York hotels (I remember staying at one of them, in Sutton Place, long after West had left). All these experiences helped him to become a novelist, though his works are generally more than merely realistic. Of his quartet of novels, the finest are the second (Miss Lonelyhearts, 1933) and the fourth (The Day of the Locust, 1939). Irving Malin has nimbly demonstrated why they are the best.

In 1935, West went to Hollywood, first to adapt Miss Lonelyhearts for the screen (as Advice to the Lovelorn). After that he wrote several other films, sometimes in collaboration. The destructiveness of Hollywood to imaginative writers who go out there is too well known to need further comment here. That West could survive the treadmill is apparent in The Day of the Locust, in every moment of its acid grotesquerie. But West couldn't survive his own bad driving; he was killed in an auto accident, along with his wife, the former Eileen McKenney. This calamity occurred a few days before Ruth McKenney's play about Eileen (My Sister Eileen) began its successful run on Broadway, another irony of the kind West would have understood.

All of his novels present a challenge: What is he really getting at? All of them are fun to read, though Miss Lonelyhearts and Day of the Locust are the most fun; they have what might be called comic grimness. The Day of the Locust projects the shabbier edges of Hollywood existence, while Miss Lonelyhearts is about a tough newspaperman assigned to take over the advice-to-the-lovelorn column, which at first amuses him; he gradually slips out of his cynicism as he eventually becomes agitated over the mawkish problems of the suffering people who wrote to "Miss Lonelyhearts" for help. This is a great American fable, superbly presented, and now examined (as West's other three books are) with acumen by Professor Malin in this outstanding book of critical interpretation.

HARRY T. MOORE

Southern Illinois University
March 2, 1972

Acknowledgments

Grateful acknowledgment is made to the following publishers for permission to quote from the following novels: Nathanael West, *Miss Lonelyhearts*, Copyright 1933 by Nathanael West © 1960 by Laura Perelman. *The Day of the Locust*, Copyright 1939 by the Estate of Nathanael West © 1966 by Laura Perelman. Reprinted by permission of New Directions Publishing Corporation and Laurence Pollinger, Limited.

Quotations from *The Dream Life of Balso Snell* and *A Cool Million* published in *The Complete Works of Nathanael West*. © 1957 by Farrar, Straus & Cudahy, Inc. Copyright 1931 by Moss and Kamin. Copyright 1933, 1934 by Nathanael West. Copyright 1939 by the estate of Nathanael West. Also reprinted in *Two Novels by Nathanael West*, originally published by Farrar, Straus and Company, Noonday Press, 1963. Reprinted by permission of Farrar, Straus & Giroux, Inc.

Nathanael West's Novels

1

Approaches to the Novels

Nathanael West is an important American novelist. His four novels—*The Dream Life of Balso Snell*; *Miss Lonelyhearts*; *A Cool Million*; and *The Day of the Locust*—take up less than 450 pages in the one-volume edition published by Farrar, Straus in 1957; but they have already compelled many critics to study them seriously. There are three critical studies—*Nathanael West: An Interpretative Study* by James F. Light (1961); *Nathanael West: The Ironic Prophet* by Victor Comerchero (1964); *The Fiction of Nathanael West: No Redeemer, No Promised Land* by Randall Reid (1967)—a critical biography—*Nathanael West: The Art of His Life* by Jay Martin (1970)—and a pamphlet in the University of Minnesota series, *Nathanael West* by Stanley Edgar Hyman (1962). At least fifty articles have been devoted to his novels.

Although there has been so much written, no critical study attempts to read the novels in a chronological way, from the opening chapter to the end. We are offered discussions of sources—Dostoevsky, William James, the French symbolists, Freud—and although these are valuable comparativist studies—I am especially impressed by Randall Reid's work—they somehow overwhelm the novels and disrupt the reading experience.[1] They assume that the text is not the last word. I believe that this is a dangerous procedure. I concentrate, therefore, upon the explication of texts, perhaps giving them more attention (especially *A Cool Million*) than they deserve.

The novels are constructed tightly. *Miss Lonelyhearts* and *The Day of the Locust*, the best ones, demand that we explore intensively images, metaphors, and symbols because they are the heart of the matter. The symbols are as important, if not more important, than characterization and theme. They incarnate the latter elements. The novels are formal designs which create their powerful effects by the accumulation of significant recurring details. They are perfectly suited to explication.

I am interested in West because he is so ambivalent. Although he creates his art with great care, as I hope to demonstrate, he does not possess a closed mind. He gives us no final solutions. When we read the last sentence of any of his novels, we are not completely relieved of the tensions and ambivalences preceding it. *Miss Lonelyhearts*, for example, concludes with: "They both rolled part of the way down the stairs." I underline "part of the way"—it symbolizes his refusal to write an easy conclusion, fixing guilt and offering rewards. Miss Lonelyhearts, Peter Doyle, and Betty are implicated in the violence—they share responsibility; they are all on the stairs. The novels reverberate with such ambiguities.

Some critics have tried to capture the sources of West's ambivalence. James F. Light claims that "the reason West's novels are involved in the Quest is his rejection of a heritage both familial and racial, that burdened West just as Joyce's heritage weighed on that great nay sayer." [2] He maintains that West is tormented by his Jewishness and his need to rebel against it. Surely Light is correct in a general way. We cannot read *The Dream Life of Balso Snell* or, for that matter, any of the other novels, without noticing the crude slurs directed toward Jewish merchants. Their names, manners, and clothing are ridiculed. But Light is simplistic in his sociological analysis. He links West, Salinger, Bellow on one page as raging for order. Although he admits that "the rage for order is hardly a Jewish monopoly," he, nevertheless, believes that he has found the key. [3]

Max F. Schulz is a better reader of Jewishness. He realizes that it lies in West's inability to "rest content in the human suspension between heavenly aspirations and earthly limitations, belief and skepticism, order and disorder. He portrays life in his novels as a conflict of inadequate imperatives offered to man by society and culture as guides to live by." [4] He views him as a religious writer seeking answers outside of the faith he knew as a child. I think that Schulz does not go far enough. He does not have the space—his chapter on West is followed by chapters on Malamud, Mailer, Salinger, et al.—to define the Jewish experience as more than "radical sophistication." He does not make much of the elements of exile, family life, head and heart, and transcendence in traditional Jewish experience. [5] He does not isolate the use of irony, parable, or dream by Jews in their art. Schulz is, however, on the right path.

The problem with reading the novels for their Jewish (or anti-Jewish?) themes and characterization is that they tend then to become sermons or texts for sermons. They are made to carry unnecessary burdens. Their careful, literary designs are partially neglected.

Several critics make them carry other burdens. They see West's ambivalence resulting from his sexual tensions. Comerchero suggests that "For West, sex was such a primary motivating force that it shaped, if it did not determine, most human behavior. At the same time, it was a force as inexplicable as any other one might choose, and also one which concretely dramatized forces beyond man's control." [6] He searches for and discovers castration, homosexuality, and Oedipal guilt in the novels (especially in *Miss Lonelyhearts*), citing many phallic details. Comerchero, following Stanley Edgar Hyman (whom he praises for his tidy reading), [7] becomes obsessive about Freudianism, and neglects to observe that psychosexual overtones are not the final clue to *Miss Lonelyhearts*. He does not heed the advice that he offers in his opening chapter: "The vague uneasiness we feel when reading West is often due to our subliminal perception of this Freudian dimension." [8]

Comerchero is so conscious of the perception that he kills it. The novels are, in the end, more than case histories. Randall Reid puts the matter concisely: "The homosexual interpretation is, then, so weak that it requires us to ignore many of [*Miss Lonelyhearts'*] details and invent others. It is also quite irrelevant to the novel's issues. Nothing in the diagnosis explains the fact of mass suffering or the reasons for Miss Lonelyhearts' response to that suffering or the ultimate failure of his mission." [9]

There is no doubt that we can read the novels psychologically, but we must remember West's own notes on *Miss Lonelyhearts*: "Psychology has nothing to do with reality nor should it be used as motivation. The novelist is no longer a psychologist. Psychology can become something much more important. The great body of case histories can be used in the way the ancient writers used their myths. Freud is your Bulfinch; you can not learn from him." [10] These notes are frequently quoted, but they remain tantalizingly obscure. West is as ambivalent toward Freud as he is toward the Jew. (He does not realize that Freudianism itself is largely Jewish in content and form.) [11] I interpret his remarks to mean that novels should take psychology for granted —it is an axiom, a given myth which is not the answer but merely the beginning. He goes beyond psychology. He refuses to give us the childhoods of Lemuel Pitkin, Balso Snell, Tod Hackett, and Miss Lonelyhearts. His heroes may remember a few incidents from their pasts, but they never stop to analyze their parents or their traumas. They exist in a kind of vacuum; their present condition is all that matters—and this condition has as much to do with religious transcendence as violent sex.

It is, of course, interesting to compare the reactions of West's heroes (much more interesting than to relate these reactions to the writer himself), but we should be tentative. I believe that narcissism is closer to the missing source of their reactions than homosexuality, castration etc.; it predates the latter. The heroes are fascinated with their bodies in such a way that they cannot cope with reality. They keep thinking about holes, wounds, deformities, and even beauties. Their bodies become totemic, holding secret and mysterious power. Their narcissism is strikingly ambiguous. They are in love-and-hate with their physical being; they would like to surrender it or, to use West's word, "dismantle it," but they cannot let go. Thus they are caught in a vicious cycle. They hate what they need to live with. This psychological phenomenon is the novelistic axiom.

West stops here. He does not inform us where the narcissism began; he omits parental training, childhood rituals of excretion, Oedipal romance. He destroys the past. At the same time he makes his heroes act strangely toward other people. Women are usually maternal (see Betty and Fay in *Miss Lonelyhearts*; Mrs. Pitkin in *A Cool Million*; or Miss McGeeney in one of her transformations in *The Dream Life of Balso Snell*) or destructive creatures (see Faye Greener in *The Day of the Locust*). Men are threatening authorities (Shrike in *Miss Lonelyhearts*, the various guides in *The Dream Life of Balso Snell*, and the police and judges in *A Cool Million*). The heroes are out of place in the adult world. Wherever they turn for comfort and instruction, they find danger. It is no wonder that they retreat into their beds (or shells or enclosures), preferring to play mentally with their own bodies. Perhaps this is the secret of the novels' endings. A wet dream (*Balso Snell*); a shooting and falling down the stairs (*Miss Lonelyhearts*); a final dismantling and martyrdom (*A Cool Million*); a hysterical laugh (*The Day of the Locust*) — these various endings rehearse the flight into sleep, dreams, the womb of self.

West's novels are childish. Although they are written with great authority, they lapse into silliness (*A Cool Million*) and exhibitionism (*The Dream Life of Balso Snell*). These lapses are often noted—what critic could neglect them?—but they are usually dismissed without analyzing their sources. I suggest that they are the clue to the shaping spirit behind all the novels. The novels deal with the fears (and rages) that an innocent child feels in the adult world; heroes vent their feelings in primitive ways—they have fits or tantrums when they discover that their bodies are mere objects to others. The fact that *The Dream Life of Balso Snell* is a closed dreamworld should alert us to this narcissistic quality.

Closed dreamworld! The phrase, once we think of it, applies to the underlying structure of all the novels. *Balso Snell* is a series of dreams-within-dreams, centering in the hero's unconscious desires for sexual fulfillment. Despite the many episodes, it returns to the adolescent wet dream as the source of the preceding art. *Miss Lonelyhearts* has many more realistic characters than the first novel, but they seem to be extreme projections of the hero; they are aspects of his tormented personality. It is impossible at times to separate Miss Lonelyhearts from Shrike or Peter Doyle. There is a dreamlike quality because events and characters are melodramatic, stylized, and self-serving. *A Cool Million* describes the American dream (the freedom to gain success), but behind this dream lies the same narcissistic desires and attitudes we have seen. Mr. Whipple, Jake Raven, Wu Fong, and Lemuel Pitkin are drawn in heavy strokes as a child would portray them. *The Day of the Locust* is set in the closed dreamworld of Hollywood. Here childish feelings are given professional status because they are the creative forces behind our movies. The novel opens with an army marching with "the jangle of iron"; the entire scene emphasizes the unreal, primitive nature.

West's novels are "on the edge." They begin with quest (or, better yet, wish-fulfillment) and end with nightmarish failure. Balso Snell dreams of completion as an artist (and man); Miss Lonelyhearts wants to save the world; Lemuel Pitkin, on a lover level of aspiration, travels extensively to find money for his mother's house; and Tod Hackett hopes to paint "The Burning of Los Angeles." These heroes are defeated. They are overwhelmed by dark violence (bred of frustration). West is shrewd enough to underline the dreams of his heroes by writing dreams-within-the-basic-dream. His novels are full of dreams—to the point that it becomes difficult to separate or define clearly the waking state. By emphasizing dreams, he compels us to realize that rationalism, sanity, and daylight thinking are less important (and creative) than the irrational dreams we share.

I believe that West writes about compulsive designs. His heroes try to plot their lives to reach the goals they have set for themselves, but they act obsessively. They do not see much of reality—only those aspects which fit or mirror their needs. Is there any difference between Miss Lonelyhearts and Ahab or John Marcher in "The Beast in the Jungle"? These three heroes—not to mention a Thomas Sutpen or William Wilson—are similar because they refuse to acknowledge the demands of others. They cannot be fully human (or grown up) insisting as they do upon their self-centered dreams of glory. West's novels are very American in their portrayal of these designs.

They resemble the romances described by Richard Chase.[12] They shy away from the full-bodied, substantial materials used by George Eliot or Jane Austen. They are flat, stylized, and nocturnal. Their very strength lies in such qualities. They refuse to accept the world as it is; they rage against it as they cry for more—for more wisdom and goodness. They want to believe in the values of everyday life—as the English novel does—but they know that such values cannot exist with certainty in a world of illusion, deception, and violence. The oddity, the narrowness, the intensity—aren't these, finally, the only clear method to capture the American experience?

West is often praised by our contemporary writers. I am thinking especially of Flannery O'Connor and John

Hawkes. Hawkes's essay, "Flannery O'Connor's Devil,"
is an important document not only for its shrewd
analysis of Miss O'Connor but for its comparison of her
novels with those of West.[13] It establishes the bonds
between West and new American Gothic represented
by her and Hawkes himself (and Purdy).[14]

Hawkes makes several significant points: "I would
propose that West and Flannery O'Connor are very
nearly alone today in their employment of the devil's
voice as vehicle for their satire or for what we may call
their true (or accurate) vision of our godless actu-
ality."[15] He believes that although the sources of their
aesthetic authority are different, both writers demolish
man's pretensions to rationality. They refuse to compro-
mise with their respective faiths (Miss O'Connor as
orthodox believer; West as atheist); they attack the
prevailing softness of our culture. Hawkes affirms their
devilish power; he suggests that they are half in love
with the violence and immorality they portray. They
are curiously ambivalent.

Hawkes makes one more point. He underlines the
comic vision of both writers—this vision violates "an-
ticipated, familiar reality" and creates a new, strange,
independent reality which is, ironically, for him a more
valid one. He insists, therefore, on their literary designs.

The essay must be read by anyone interested in contemporary American fiction. It tells us that West's
influence is great because his novels represent a tense,
artistic attempt to redeem our culture (and personalities) through extreme patterns. These patterns, as I
have maintained, must be viewed in literary terms. They
go beyond Freudian reductionism (although they begin
with narcissistic axioms) because they are shaped by
West's consciously symbolist imagination.

I find in rereading my first chapter of *New American
Gothic* that almost everything I say there can apply to
West. I refer specifically to my comments on the dreamlike nature of Gothic. West employs many opposing
symbols—the house and the voyage (or "field-trip"—

to use his word); the actor and the spectator; the real
and the unreal et al. These couples establish the frame
of reference for his narcissistic heroes. Because Miss
Lonelyhearts or Tod Hackett cannot solve his religious-
psychological problems (who can?), he tends to have
double vision. He is unable to see reality clearly; he
tends to view it as a set of ambivalent forces. The
objects which surround him (aside from his body) become terrifying. Thus Miss Lonelyhearts cannot merely
accept his room and forget about it. It gets out of
control; it suddenly becomes imbued with all sorts of
meaning (enclosure, womb, tomb), and these meanings shake him because he cannot take a stand. He
cannot commit himself to one meaning. His ambivalence, of course, is much greater when he has to cope
with various metaphysical symbols. Christ disturbs him
more than his room, but the two externals share this
perplexing quality.

Rooms: the "horse" in *The Dream Life of Balso
Snell*; the newspaper office in *Miss Lonelyhearts*; the
interior decoration in *A Cool Million*; the frame-devices
in *The Day of the Locust*. These basic rooms are
echoed in so many other symbolic structures that West
almost gives us the "other voices, other rooms" of
Capote. The important thing is that they are all
haunted. Balso feels trapped (as he is in his own body),
and he cannot get out. When he journeys forth, he is
destroyed by violent, frenetic movement.

Voyage: all the novels are built on a journey as the
epigraph to *The Dream Life of Balso Snell* would lead
us to believe: "After all, my dear fellow, life, Anaxagoras has said, is a journey." But the journey is "to the
end of night" because the heroes do not move steadily.
Their "pilgrim's progress" is interfered with by repe-
titions, coincidences, and crowds. Any page of West's
novels stresses such unbalanced movement. I need only
cite the army "jumbled together in bobbing disorder"
at the beginning of *The Day of the Locust* to point the
way.

I have compulsively stressed unclear vision of the heroes (not of West who sees clearly and independently). This vision also functions symbolically. Balso perceives "strange foreshortenings" (he is describing the girl cripples) throughout his adventures; Miss Lonelyhearts stares at the crucifix and "it becomes a bright fly"; Lemuel Pitkin has a glass eye; and Tod is a painter who uses fantastic, deformed models to get at reality. The novels are visionary, but like those of new American Gothic, they propose that epiphanies are duplicitous, warped, and somehow unbelievable.

I have mentioned three recurring symbols—there are, of course, many more examples which I will note in my explications—to imply that West is the spiritual father (or brother) of the writers I have discussed in *New American Gothic*. He is important not only as an independent figure but as a traditional, inspirational guide to younger writers.

Now that I have perhaps belabored these various comparisons, I propose to turn directly to West's novels. They stand alone, finally, as powerful, complex works of art.

The Dream Life of Balso Snell

Perhaps the best way to get into West's first novel, *The Dream Life of Balso Snell* (1931), is by exploring the implications of the title. We are given the union of dream and life—there is no indication that we can (or should) separate the two worlds. Life as dream; dream as life—we cannot be sure about truth; things are so problematical and fuzzy that their very existence becomes unreal. Balso Snell is an appropriately fantastic name which manages to suggest testicularity, circularity, violence (especially in the way the "sn" sound cuts the "o" sound), and clownlike behavior. The title is, then, a clue to the themes, images, and structures of the entire novel.

The first two paragraphs reinforce these suggestions:

> While walking in the tall grass that has sprung up around the city of Troy, Balso Snell came upon the famous wooden horse of the Greeks. A poet, he remembered Homer's ancient song and decided to find a way in.
>
> On examining the horse, Balso found that there were but three openings: the mouth, the navel, and the posterior opening of the alimentary canal. The mouth was beyond his reach, the navel proved a cul-de-sac, and so, forgetting his dignity, he approached the last. O Anus Mirabilis!

West places us (and Balso) in an odd environment—first tall grass; then Troy; then the wooden horse—

which although described clearly, alarms us because it is so foreign. We lose our footing. The "famous wooden horse" may reassure us by its glibness, but it suddenly changes from a safe cliché into a threatening, new object with holes. Openings, like O's, invite movement —however, such movement can be restricted as is obvious in the next-to-last sentence. I stress the openings not only because they introduce West's obsessive interest in the individual body but also in "the world's body"—the environment we must enter at our own risk. It is easy to forget that he is metaphysical in the attempt to be physical—he realizes that the dream life of Balso Snell fuses body and spirit, the natural and supernatural. Poets, he reminds us, use and transform alimentary (or elementary) openings to make miracles.

In the horse Balso discovers mysterious writings which he can decipher only after great difficulty. These inspire him. (Throughout the novel he obeys the muse.) He makes a song. It contains references to the body ("navel," "anus," "tongues," "belly," "feet"); to religion (the Deity and Mary are mentioned twice); and to art (Giotto). But the underlying principle uniting the three themes of art, religion, and physicality seems to be the circle. The song begins with the word "round," moves to "buttons," "wheels," "round belly," "perfect circles," "brimming goblet," and "holes." It is possible to claim that Balso (and West) is merely sexually oriented, looking everywhere for the good opening, but as we look closely at the circle, we realize that it symbolizes desired perfection. Art, the body, and religion try to give us perfection, immortality, and eternity —they persuade us to give up our special angles of vision, our lines of tension. But they lie, according to West. They merely disguise pain and anxiety. They are fakes. Thus it is interesting to note that when Balso finishes his song, he makes fun of it (as it makes fun of itself) by calling it A *Voyage Through the Hole in the Mundane Millstone*. The holes are determinedly not holy. (The temptation to pun is too great to resist, especially because West does so constantly.) [1] The "Phoenix Excrementi" "eat themselves, digest themselves, and give birth to themselves by evacuating their bowels. . . ." in a vicious parody of perfect, circular movement.

Balso meets a tour guide after he ends his tale of the Excrementi. The guide is the first of the authority images in the novel (and in all of West's works.) He is proud, defiant, and wise. "Mind your manners, foreigner. If you don't like it here, why don't you go back where you came from." [2] He narrates a story—it is the first story-within-the-story, the first circle-within-the-circle. A traveler, we are told, observes a snake enter the lower part of Appolonious's body. He informs the sage, who merely replies that the snake lives there. The traveler, now convinced that he is speaking to the real Appolonious, asks to see the snake and the opening. Although the guide does not explain his tale of "visitors," Balso calls it "perfect, perfect!" What does the tale (another pun) mean? Apparently visitors—that is the traveler, Balso, and any artist—must inspect activity and passivity, lines and circles. Only then can he achieve the wisdom of Appolonious, the ability to be at peace with threatening snake-like existence. The guide narrates other stories (to help Balso narrate this one?), but he falls for low comedy.

Finally he makes two important points. He screams: "I am a Jew. I'm a Jew. A Jew!" He proclaims his identity, but he does not really inform us about the reasons for his identification. The proclamation is made to appear ridiculous, hysterical, and mad. Why? Balso (or West) does not give any reasons. We have to supply them tentatively. The Jew is feared because he accepts the impossibility of grace—it is nonexistent for him—and the probability of irreconcilable earthly differences. He refuses to surrender dialectical thinking for easy circularity. He is full of tension; he needs no perfect circle to sustain him on earth. Balso rushes to assure the guide that he "has nothing against the Jews," but he really does. They won't conform to his quest and obsession for circularity and (w)holeness.[3] When he quotes Doughty's epigram, "the semites are like to a man sitting in a cloaca to the eyes, and whose brows touch heaven," he makes them share his own anal obsessions and his desire to possess heaven excrementally. He makes them share his rage and passivity.

I think that Balso's discussion immediately following his anti-Semitic remarks emphasizes the truth of my suggestions. He again refers to art in circular terms: "A circle has neither a beginning nor an end. A circle has no feet. If we believe that nature is a circle, then we must also believe that there are no feet in nature." Balso wants to flee from feet and excrement—his persistent remarks overcompensate for his fears—because they represent beginnings and ends, sources of tension. He grasps at perfection, hating those, like the Jews, who accept the lines of history and body. Although he may follow his creator, West, in stressing the beauty of circles, he secretly understands that he can only dream such beauty. And his dreams turn into nightmares—the circles eat themselves and him. They are determinedly cannibalistic.[4] Perhaps the swift ending of this section with the guide resembles the dream turning into nightmare: Balso tears loose with "a violent twist."

Next he meets a man, "naked except for a derby in which thorns were sticking, who was attempting to crucify himself with thumb tacks." Maloney is another spiritual guide, but he is a Catholic mystic. Of course, he is an object of ridicule, especially as he tells his story of "Saint Puce, a great martyred member of the vermin family." Saint Puce was a flea who lived and died beneath the arm of Christ. He had two mothers, Christ and the winged creature. (His mysterious birth echoes the birth of Christ.) He was martyred after Christ died because he had no flesh to nourish him. The "unconquerable worm" bit him. This morbid, wild story again reflects Balso's obsessive concern with the body. Flesh, blood, and "much-shaven armpits" revolt and fascinate him—they reveal that he will die on Calvary. They say "memento mori." His future art (like religion) will not save him; the perfect circle will not appear. Balso calls Maloney morbid. "Stop sniffing mortality. Play games," he screams. But even the games that he and West play, rage helplessly against mortality. Their laughter as in "Take cold showers" does not lessen decay because it is so conscious and willful. Balso again runs away. These continual movements are desperate. (The entire novel is filled with exits and entrances; it becomes in this respect a symbol of "the world's body." We come and go; we refuse to stand still —according to West—because stasis represents some kind of death.)

From Maloney the Areopagite, another useless, threatening father, to a boy hiding a diary! John Gilson keeps a diary and crime journal to please Miss McGeeney, his teacher. (Another circular device!) These works of art are, as we would suspect, full of violence, rage, and despair.

John starts the new year, hoping that he can discover the Real. "A Real that I could know with my senses. A Real that would wait for me to inspect it as a dog inspects a dead rabbit." (Notice the dead animal imagery. Reality in West is always mortal; it makes him long for immortal unreality.) John hopes to find the Real through disguise and art; he now writes a Crime Journal within the journal in which he gets to the bottom of existence. It is more natural for him because he can order things here. He will make a perfect world through circular reasoning: "Order is the test of sanity. Her emotions and thoughts are disordered. Mine are arranged, valued, placed." Such insanity becomes sanity —at least for a while. Things change. John now regards himself as insane.

In the longest entry of the Crime Journal, John views himself as an underground man, a Raskolnikov.[5] (Even his attempts to find the Real are tinged by literature. He cannot break through the body or the word.) His

imagination leads to hallucination. But such enchant-
ment with shadows is fruitless because he is aware that
he is hallucinating or as he writes, he attempts to "trace
with the point of a pencil the shadow of the tracing
pencil." He would like to blot out all consciousness,
but this act would remove him further from the Real.
He secretly courts death; he murders others so that he
will not kill himself. John (or the narrator of the Crime
Journal) purchases a knife to attack an old man. The
murder is oddly sexual. John's genitals are "tight and
hard, like a dog's or an archaic Greek statue's." (Murder
is also linked to art here.) He caresses his breasts like
a young girl "who suddenly becomes conscious of her
body on a hot afternoon." He changes sex, posturing
before sailors. These violent transformations mirror the
transformations in the entire dream life of Balso Snell.
They reveal that metaphysical rage is an attempt to flee
the body, to fight the lines (phallic?) that limit movement. John is against nature, knowing all the while that
such combat is the most natural thing in the world. He
has split consciousness. He is doomed by (and through)
himself.

John tells us that laughter is more terrible than tears.
His victim is associated with laughing: "He was laughing to himself. His laughter made me laugh." Perhaps
the murder is, then, an attempt to destroy laughter, to
kill that quality which separates us from beasts. But
John learns that he cannot refrain from his own peculiar
kind of joking. He always notes the irony of his situation
—murder does not help to solve his problems, especially
his desire to touch Reality.

The exchange between Balso and John (an interlude)
reinforces these ironies. Balso admits that he likes
the Journal for its psychological interest but wonders
about its art. (We will ask similar questions about the
entire novel.) John replies that he cares little about art;
he writes to seduce his English teacher who likes underground works. "Read less and play baseball," counsels
Balso. Art creates sickness—the association is ironic

because it appears in a book which reverses the circuit, trying to create art out of sickness. And Balso cannot really evaluate John; his criticism is always self-serving and narcissistic—shall we call it sick? The reversals lend an air of unreality to the realistic exchanges (to the spaces between artworks). The Real is ironically veiled by circular analysis.

The pamphlet which is read now by Balso is written by a narrator who mourns the death of his beloved Saniette. The narrator looks "into the bowels" of his compassion (another excremental vision?) but cannot cry. He is "cardboard and tin"—a stylized, metallic creature like all of the characters we encounter. He considers Death, Love, and Beauty impossible subjects to think about because they are tinged (or dirtied) by literary associations. The Real thus becomes Art—a parodic circle which, instead of being as pure as Balso wishes, reinforces the tensions we face.

Saniette is seen in perspective as the audience for the performer-narrator: "Her casualness excited me so that I became more and more desperate in my performances." He becomes a clown assuming "funny" poses for her. This art—is it any different from John's journal to seduce his teacher or Balso's dreams to make himself attractive?—is compulsively narcissistic. He compares himself to the "Inornata," a dull-colored bird, who seduces the female by building "a house of flowers." [6] He loves himself by loving Saniette. Another vicious cycle?

By going in circles, the narrator informs us that he laughs at all emotions, except the need to please. He evens laughs at the laugh. Therefore he moves farther away from his goal of understanding; he is trapped in an infinity of mirrors. [7] He sees so much that he is blind. In a hotel bedroom with Saniette (as he remembers the scene) he beats her, hoping to get out of his skin. (Sadism and art are linked again.) But the beating doesn't help because he keeps thinking of his body. The "materials of life—wood, glass, wool, skin—are rubbing against my sty, my cold sore and my pimples; rubbing in such a way as not to satisfy the itch or convert irritation into active pain, but so as to increase the size of the irritation, magnify it and make it seem to cover everything—hysteria, despair." The active pain lasts for a few seconds before it unfortunately turns into "monotonous" irritation. How can the narrator perfect the pain and make it last eternally? The question cannot be answered, especially by Saniette and the clerk.

But the narrator persists in his quest for perfection. He mentions de Sade—to no avail. It is only when he creates metaphors (art) that he comes closer to eternal pain. (His strategy mirrors West's novelistic process.) He thinks of his predicament—torn between irritation (life, the body) and pain (death, the spiritual loss of consciousness)—in terms of "myself and the chauffeur within me." The chauffeur is large, ugly, and excremental. (His shoes are covered with "animal ordure.") We would expect him to represent unthinking violence but we are shocked when he is said to be "The Desire to Procreate." By linking ugliness and procreation, the narrator unbalances us; the dream life becomes nightmarish once more as wish-fulfillment (at least for most people!) suddenly becomes unbearable. The process is even more complicated. The chauffeur—a "cloth-covered devil"—dominates the narrator; he almost "rapes" him. Thus the pain wins—if only for the moment of metaphor. But irritation returns as the metaphor is rationalized and understood.

The chauffeur is linked to Saniette. Although the narrator uses metaphor, he needs an audience to appreciate it. He must break through his own body; he must seduce others. Saniette is the desired (and undesired) audience. But she, of course, does not understand. The exquisite pain the narrator wants to capture turns again to irritation because of the "sensitive yet hardboiled" Saniette. He would like to kill her, but he needs her laughter. What is left? The narrator thinks of her (and the audience she represents) drowned in excrement: "In case the audience should misunderstand and align itself on the side of the artist, the ceiling of the theatre will be made to open and cover the occupants with tons of loose excrement." Anality becomes a metaphor of murder. (And vice versa!) Look closely at the sentence. The narrator doesn't want the audience (or the loved one) to share his art (or procreation); such community threatens his selfish existence.[8] At the same time he desires union, hoping to exploit it for his own ends. The tension is so great that he wishes for a sign—a miracle, if you will—to resolve the matter. Excrement is the sign—it covers everything! But even it lacks perfection. The deluge stops and we are now told that the audience can gather in "the customary charming groups." The play goes on; so does irritating life.

So does Balso Snell. After reading the pamphlet, he throws it away with a sigh because he can find no answers. (John Gilson is thus thrown away—another "guide" fails to enlighten him.) He treats himself with platitudes—the war, communism, the movies. They comfort him for the moment, especially when they are echoed by a "slim young girl." The girl washes her "hidden charms"—this interesting phrase suggests the easy, convenient platitudes as well as the anxiety-provoking mysteries. It is two-faced, paradoxically holding creative and destructive tendencies.[9] When the girl calls upon him to feel "the warm knife of thought," she reinforces the tension. We don't usually associate knives and warmth (or knives and progress) but in the dream world of Balso Snell, oppositions and paradoxes rise to the surface. Wish-fulfillment and nightmare marry. It is, of course, no surprise that the girl turns into a "middle aged woman dressed in a mannish suit." Sexuality is duplicitous and "hidden."

Miss McGeeney, as she is now called, is a writer and teacher. She informs Balso that she is writing a biography of a biographer of a biographer. . . . The circle reasserts itself, but it is laughed at. It is not the symbol of perfection but of tedious uselessness. The literary chain does not lead to new truths. It suggests that West is playing games with us throughout the novel. Although he uses a circular structure (the guide recurs; the story-within-the-story-within-the-story recurs), he realizes that its "hidden charm" may lie in its irritation. He wants us to be bored and annoyed—to be caught in his circular trap. He wants us to feel the claustrophobia of art (and the body). He succeeds.

The matter is even more complicated: Miss McGeeney describes Perkins's face. (He is the subject of her biography.) It is "dominated by his nose." The nose— did West know Gogol's story?—resembles the "warm knife of thought" mentioned earlier.[10] It is also a comforting weapon to assault reality (and/or to measure it). It is almost superhuman as it smells "the caress of velvet and the strength of iron." It cuts across boundaries of sense; it defies limits. There is only one problem. Perkins's nose is so powerful that it becomes vicious. Reality is discovered only through the sense of smell. Everything is reduced to a circle or a "tread-mill." Perkins is locked in the circle; he can only move along the circumference. He tries to make the circumference into an infinite straight line, by moving rapidly "from simplicity to perversion." He runs up and down the ladder of smell; he finds in the odors of his wife's body "an architecture and an aesthetic, a music and a mathematic." Or so Miss McGeeney thinks. We must remember that she creates Perkins (as Balso creates her). Her dream is to make Perkins become a champion or a deity who rises above the nose (and reality). She wants him to be eternal. Her reasoning is satirized by Balso. He hits her in the gut; he brings her down to earth. He does more—by throwing her into the fountain, he cleanses her perceptions of excremental wish-fulfillment. He gives her a "cold shower" to remind her—and himself—of tense mortality.[11] Another interlude (or dream-within-dream) ends in frustration and anger.

Balso Snell walks away as he realizes that the wooden

horse (the womb of deception?) is inhabited solely by "writers in search of an audience." He is determined not to meet another guide who will explain the meanings of life and art; he will remain a loner. Balso courts seclusion but he is married to his dreams. Now he dreams of another art-palace, Carnegie Hall—in the lobby are crowded many "beautiful girl-cripples." Although most men are disturbed by their "strange forms," he loves such deformities as short legs, humps, and wall-eyes. He finds delight in them. Why? Can he see himself in the girl-cripples? Does he identify with their strange forms? Are they all beautiful losers? It is hard to give definite answers to these irritating questions; nevertheless, it seems likely that Balso continues in his old pattern of attraction and repulsion in terms of his own narcissism. He is attracted by the insane and the ugly, seeing in them his own "strange forms" of body and spirit; he is repelled by the others who do not fit into his dreams. He is constantly torn by the desire to be master and slave. He wants to dominate the cripples —it would signify his own strength of character—but once they change and become normal or healthy, he fears their domination. The entire novel, then, is a dream of sadomasochism. But we would deform it even more if we were to stop at this level (this part of the "wooden horse"), because as I have suggested, West uses the physical (or psychosexual) as a metaphor of the metaphysical. In the passage involving the girl-cripples, he employs such phrases as "the niceness of perfection." Balso Snell, we can say, desires imperfection because it demonstrates that there is no grace, no way out of the "strange forms" of his existence. He is irritated when changes—or promises of perfection— occur to upset his world.

In his dream of the girl-cripples—notice how effectively the hyphenated phrase captures the tension of opposites—he spies one who is extremely "tall in spite of her enormous hump." The Lepi, as he calls her, inspires him. He will love her so much that her sores will be rose-ripe. He will master her deviations (demonstrating to himself that she is more beautiful than someone else).

The Lepi is attracted to Balso—how could she fail to be?—and thinks of "being subdued by a male." Salvation seems to be near. Love can be the answer—the perfect circle? The Lepi calls Love "sacred" and "strange." But Balso is afraid to go to the limit; he must stay close to earth. He debases Love; he tosses it into excrement. Thus he can understand and master it.

The Lepi wants him to kill Beagle Darwin. (Love and violence are, of course, partners in the entire dream life.) Beagle Darwin! What a suggestive name! The Beagle is a sad-looking animal; Darwin signifies the survival of the best. The name is paradoxical (animal-man, victim-master). Beagle Darwin is, appropriately enough, a poet who has betrayed the Lepi (now called Janey Davenport!). He therefore mirrors Balso, who is trying to do the same thing. The matter becomes more complicated when we see Janey and Balso as doubles (which they are because Janey is "dreamed" by Balso). Beagle, Janey, Balso—all characters share the desire to escape from their claustrophobic predicaments. Janey gives Balso two letters to read. The circle repeats itself—the letters resemble the anecdotes of the guides; the pamphlet of John Gilson; and the biography of Perkins written by Miss McGeeney. *Not only do the characters merge—their artistic creations also come together.*[12] There is no "otherness," no way out of the individual mind of Balso (or West). The novel apparently whirls about from adventure to adventure, but it remains fixed. Perhaps its tension can be suggested best by remembering the ironic epigraph: "After all, my dear fellow, life, Anaxagoras has said, is a journey." Balso moves but stands still; "progress" gives way to stasis. (The epigraph even mirrors this—we expect profundity at the end of the sentence, but we are trapped in cliché!)

The first letter begins with "Darling Janey." And the clichés continue from here. Beagle writes a letter-within-the-letter, making believe that he is "pregnant, un-married, unloved, lonely, watching the laughing crowds hurry past. . . ." By becoming Janey, he (and West) can be two-sided—his sadomasochistic tendencies flourish in "strange forms." Thus when he cries "I want to keep a hard, outside surface towards the world, and a soft, inner side for him . . . ," he permits us to realize that he is hard and soft, strong and weak. The weakness dominates this act of ventriloquism, especially when he writes that he is a misfit—an unexplainable joke—or that he wraps his predicament around himself, "snuggling into it. . . ." Perhaps the most effective simile occurs when Beagle-Janey writes about death. Death "is still like putting on a wet suit—shivery." We don't usually associate wetness and death (except in dreams of drowning!), and we are struck with a shivery quality at the unexpected turn.

West is too much of an artist to allow us to be comforted by simple psychology. We move swiftly from the odd similies to outright cliché. After the wet suit, Beagle-Janey muses about abortion and ugliness without any tense figures of speech: "he is like all men; he wants only one thing." Parody brings us down to earth. There is a letdown. Although it is easy to condemn West for not staying at one level, we may misread his intended effects. Is he trying to demonstrate that no matter how much we try to escape from life (through artistic figures), we are stuck inside the horse? What more effective way to incarnate flight and entrapment than in the very language of the letter? I raise these questions, but I am unsure of the answers. Perhaps I want to see more subtlety than West offers.

Beagle's first letter ends as he returns to his own identity. After a one-sentence interlude in which we return to the "real" Balso and Janey, we read the second letter. Here Beagle informs his "darling Janey" that he did his best to keep their characters "scientific and just" in the first letter. Now he will describe—to "even the score"—how "I would have received your death."

But first he makes an interesting comment about literature and life. He has spent his life in books; he has
become a book: "This literary coloring is a protective
one—like the brown of the rabbit or the checks of the
quail—making it impossible for me to tell where
literature ends and I begin." Literature (art in general)
is seen as an enclosure or skin which protects one from
life. It is a wooden horse, if you will, or an unnatural
body. It is comforting, offering shelter; it is also re-
strictive. It is, to use another one of the controlling
metaphors of the novel, a deceptive circle. Literature
destroys identity, especially when it becomes obsessive.
Beagle's predicament is that he doesn't "begin" or
"end"—he is stuck in excremental words. (He resembles the Excrementi or the playgoers who are
drowned.) But he is even more lost than they because
he is serious about words. They are all that he has.
They create (if only momentarily) and destroy him.
His situation is ironic because he knows that he should
do something. But he continues writing letters!

Beagle starts where he left off in his last letter. He
views Janey's corpse (after her fall from the hotel
window). He feels guilty. He wonders what he should
have done. Should he have torn his clothes? Prayed?
Wept? Beagle is, of course, so enclosed in art that he
cannot let go. He regards Janey as a muse, not a
person.

Her last words especially mystify him. The catch-
words of disillusion echo in his mind: Life is "empty,
rotten, and trifling"; Love is a "lure, a gimcrack, a
kickshaw." What are the proper words? Beagle does not
stop. He sees suicide itself as "arty": Goethe, the Soul,
the Quest. The associations rush past, drowning (the
image recurs!) the human, quirky response.

Beagle stops the flow by thinking of clown. Janey
and he are viewed as clowns full of pity and irony. It is
the mixture of the two qualities which fascinates him
(and West). Whenever pity threatens to dominate the
stage, there is great anguish. By pitying someone else,

we recognize human limitations. We are thrown back upon our mortal boundaries (or lines). We cannot really accept these; we must lash out with irony to affirm that we are more than human. Irony liberates us—at least momentarily. Then we feel guilty. Beagle's psychological tensions express themselves in dream-symbolism. He sees the world as audience and performer. He wants the spectators to respond to his clowning; at the same time he hates their power and respect. (Remember Saniette.) He is so ambivalent (loving and hating them because he identifies unconsciously with them) that he acts. He forgets himself; he becomes unreal. His face changes into a mask. This artistic escape is frustrating —it helps to limit true feeling—and when Beagle returns to the dressing room, he makes "the faces that won't come off with the grease paint. . . ."

Death is a joke. Janey is an arty clown (killing herself for the same old clichés). We repeat ourselves. Where can Beagle turn? He hopes for burial (another drowning) in an ivory tower; he longs to play the role of "buffoon of the New Eternities"; he desires to feign Hamlet-like madness. Such dreams of glory are ways out of the all-enclosing nightmare. Although Beagle even creates a play involving himself as "B. Hamlet Darwin" versus the patrons, he cannot get far. He is fixed in pity and irony.

He and West really want transcendence—some way out of the horse. They desperately seek metamorphosis. Dionysus, Christ—the deities who are resurrected inspire and mock them because they know any religion is an opiate. Beagle cannot be godlike; he is too covered with "slime and foul blood" to purify himself. Thus he hates Christ for cruel deception. (Another ambivalent reaction.) Perhaps he identifies Christ with the supreme audience. Although he wants to reach the audience, he can never achieve this goal. He is trapped on stage! The distance is so great that it threatens his well-being. Beagle raises his hand as though to bless the customers and waiter; he murmurs "my children." He pities them (and himself) because when they compete with Christ, they cannot win salvation.[13]

He does not stop here. His pity must be destroyed by irony; sympathy must yield to cruelty. His spiritual health is at stake. Beagle climaxes his tear-jerker routine by holding aloft "an Ivory Tower, a Still White Bird, The Holy Grail, the Nails, the Scourge, the Thorns, and a piece of the True Cross." These symbols are debased and mocked, but the very fact that they are, signifies their secret power. They are attractive enough to be destroyed.

Balso awakes and finds Miss McGeeney, the biographer of Samuel Perkins, sitting beside him. She informs him that Beagle Darwin is imaginary; he is merely a character in the novel she is writing. Our feelings toward Beagle change: we are separated from life; we lose sight of his problems as we are caught in West's artistic trap. This very condition parallels, of course, the ideas expressed in the two letters and once we realize the similarity, we recognize the communion we share. We are divided between sympathy (for such real problems as suicide) and irony.

The changes continue. Miss McGeeney is "a fine figure of a woman," not the mannish creature we have met previously. She is so attractive to Balso that he is reborn (like Christ and Dionysus?) and exclaims "Oh!" The passionate "Oh!" is immediately modified by West: "His mouth formed an O with lips torn angry in laying duck's eggs from a chicken's rectum." [14] The statement is strikingly vulgar and shocking. West refuses to allow passion to break through. By relating "Oh!" to O, he mixes romance and art with excrement, and proclaims our inability to get out of filth, out of the world's body. He catches us in a dirty circle.

Miss McGeeney screams to him that she is really his true love from the past. She becomes warmly moist. They leave the café and find themselves in the park ready for sexual play. Balso stands over her willing body and lectures on his compulsively held subjects. His lectures are psychologically fitting at this point—they signify his fear of getting out of narcissistic patterns. They climax the various metaphysical tensions in the entire novel.

Balso regards Miss McGeeney (now Mary!) as the audience. He performs, like Beagle, so that he will not have to show real feelings. He acts ambivalently. Superficially, he tries to convert her to sex; unconsciously, he hates her willingness. He lectures her so that he will not have to perform sexually.[15] First he considers the political aspect of sex. Through sex Miss McGeeney can gain Liberty from the restraints of Dogma. It is ironic that Balso forgets his own slavery to dogmatic assertion without action and his totalitarian rule over others. Beware of those who use Liberty for their own ends! (West's warning is especially clear in *A Cool Million*.)

The same tensions exist in the "philosophical aspects of the proposed act." Balso claims that because Nature has given her "a few organs capable of giving pleasure," Mary should use them. Pleasure is the only good; sex is a sacrament. Here we see his attempt to revitalize religious feeling—if Christ doesn't exist, Dionysus does and he urges us to be fruitful. The logic is a bit weak— the assumptions—Nature urges us to sex as the only good; there are no limits on our pleasure—are psychologically motivated. Again we feel that Balso is speaking for (and to) himself, not recognizing the irony of his situation.

Art is given as a reason for sex: "In my bed, love, you will find new themes, new interpretations, new experiences." Mary can learn about love—is it only physiological? is it an "all-consuming fire"? She is not told how one experience can teach so much (or how it can be transformed into art).

Balso is also unclear when he turns to the "Time-argument." Why, first of all, does he separate it from the "philosophical aspects" he has already mentioned? Does he devote so much space to this argument (his final one) to emphasize its importance? These questions are not easily answered. Balso simply rushes into usual metaphor, maintaining that time kills our capacity to enjoy sex—we must seize the day! He uses such words as "dust," "fade," "rose"—it is as if he is too tired of life and art to create new visions of temporality. Only when he characterizes life as a "bubble" does he show some originality. "Bubble" reminds us again that we are caught in a circle—any attempt to rush out of the circle means death. Thus the passage really suggests two kinds of death—resigned (passive acceptance of the circle) and active (a violent breakthrough). Some choice!

After Balso delivers his pep talk to Mary (more to himself), he falls "to the ground beside his beloved." The flatness; the clichés; the coyness—we get them all so that their love is parodied. Their souls and bodies are destroyed by words. West is so deliberately literary here that he forces us to condemn art and choose life. But we remember the way he has sneered at life through-out this novel, and we are not enthusiastic about the choice. We are left with empty O's—zero.[16]

Abruptly the tone changes (as the language becomes more intense). West now proclaims sex as a miracle "made manifest"—"The Two became One." Opposites are married: "priest and the god, the immolation, the sacrificial rite, the libation offered to ancestors. . . ." But even in this lengthy, uplifting vision we are finally left with "the Spirit of Public School 86, the last ferry that leaves for Weehawken at seven." Nothing is sacred; everything is sacred. Between these poles—so we are left with Two, not One!—lie the answers.

We have forgotten one thing in this sexual interlude. It is a dream-within-a dream. The miracle, if it occurs, is make-believe and man-made. West cannot allow us the freedom of getting out. Although he has underlined the poetry of love, he now takes us back to earth—to the mechanics of decay. Balso and Mary disappear; they are not resurrected. The solitary body is finally in command, performing "the evolution of love with . . .

sureness." Abstractions—Home, Love, Art—are forgotten in Balso's wet dream.

The last three paragraphs of the novel leave us with
a mechanical object (the body) which performs within
controlled limits of activity:

> An army moved in his body, an eager army of
> hurrying sensations. These sensations marched at
> first methodically and then hysterically, but always
> with precision. The army of his body commenced a
> long intricate drill, a long involved ceremony. A
> ceremony whose ritual unwound and manoeuvered
> itself with the confidence and training of chemicals
> acting under the stimulus of a catalytic agent.
>
> His body screamed and shouted as it marched and
> uncoiled; then, with one heaving shout of triumph, it
> fell back quiet.
>
> The army that a moment before had been thunder-
> ing in his body retreated slowly—victorious, relieved.[17]

The body is not free—like art and religion it is controlled by outside forces. It is a slave. It can only act
within limits. Although its movements are precise, they
are not artistic or passionate. "The long involved ceremony" does not resemble the ceremonies previously
mentioned (those involving Christ and Dionysus or
artist and muse). It is flat, chemical, irritating. It does
not offer ecstatic release—a way out of the circle. It
merely affirms static frustration. Thus it is fitting for
West to end ironically with a momentary victory for
the body—he knows that defeat follows victory, especially for an mechanized army.

Most critics of *The Dream Life of Balso Snell* regard
it as an uneven novel and apprentice work. I also find
that it is unsuccessful because it surrenders to its controlling metaphors. It repeats itself—life as repetition;
no exit from the circle; story-within-story. West uses
imitative form. I give him credit for imaginatively trying
to fuse life and art. By writing a circular novel about
circles, he tries to demonstrate that he is angry at life

and art. He expects more—ecstasy!—from both, but he doesn't get it. It is ironic, then, that critics see this first novel as a literary exercise or joke; they do not recognize that West is using words to alert us to flesh (and excrement). He wants words to bleed, not to be coldly mechanical, but he knows that they can't.[18] They are trapped within themselves; they are our spiritual brothers. They also inspire pity and irony.

Miss Lonelyhearts

In *Miss Lonelyhearts* (1933) West is still concerned with the dream life (the wish to escape from reality) but he does not completely use the circular, repetitive, and surrealistic structure of his first novel. He writes a more conventional work—there are chapters, a tight development of plot and character.[1]

The novel begins with the chapter "Miss Lonelyhearts, help me, help me." "Help" is, perhaps, the most significant word because it alerts us to the basis of the hero's behavior. He wants to help the world (including himself) achieve something better. His dream is to relieve suffering—at least he thinks so. He is not concerned with art—unless one thinks of his columns of advice—but with life. Of course, as the novel progresses, he tries to shape events and characters (as did Balso Snell) and his artful arrangements become more and more destructive.

Miss Lonelyhearts is sitting at his desk in this first chapter and stares at "a piece of white cardboard." The two actions—sitting and staring—are characteristic: he is passive and unmoving, but he is actively searching for something. He is a paradoxical combination of passivity and activity—he is unbalanced, alternating (as we shall note) between two poles or attitudes, uncertain about where he belongs. The white cardboard is interesting. In the first sentence it appears to be empty—waiting for his activity. It is a blank tablet, perhaps a symbol of the blankness of his life. The second sentence startles us somewhat because we learn that the white cardboard is covered with a prayer. Prayers, of course, dominate the novel because they help to blot out blankness. The prayer has been written by "Shrike the feature editor." Although we do not know Shrike yet, we are unnerved by his name, which uncannily combines shrike (a bird of prey) and shriek (a cry for help). (When we think of prey, we also think of pray.) [2] West is surely punning here; again he wants to alert us to the paradoxical, ironic, two-faced quality of life. By combining shrike and shriek, he prepares us for the inversions which will later overwhelm us. "Feature editor"—the editor is someone who has the final word; he can change things; he can eliminate the words of Miss Lonelyhearts. The prayer is strange: not only is it italicized but it also spaced out in the text. (Throughout the novel West uses italicized passages to dramatize and set apart letters, lectures, and prayers.) It is addressed to Miss L (significantly, the Lonelyhearts has been cut —Shrike does this to Miss Lonelyhearts, the man, as well as the name), and it asks for divine nourishment and help. The word *help* is repeated three times, but it is done in such a manner as to affirm the complete ineffectuality of Miss L. It is an attack, not a plea. It destroys help. Thus it also reinforces the paradoxical nature of the opening chapter.

Miss Lonelyhearts is still "working on his leader." (Does West mean us to consider a pun on "leader"? Is he suggesting that Miss Lonelyhearts tries to build his own leadership?) He is composing clichés of comfort, telling his readers that "Life *is* worthwhile." But he finds it impossible to continue. He resembles Beagle Darwin (or, for that matter, any of the writers in *The Dream Life of Balso Snell*) in his frustration. He also wants to achieve the artistic dream of mastering reality through words, but he cannot find the right, pure ones. The words he chooses are dirtied by common usage. He hates them because they cannot redeem him (or be redeemed). His predicament echoes the writers of letters. These letters are full of clichés of suffering—they are so real that they frustrate him; they remind him of his creative failure.

There are three letters in the opening chapter.[3] (They take up as much space as any of Miss Lonelyheart's actions—they are the structures in which he finds himself enclosed.) The first letter is from "Sick-of-it-all." Like Miss Lonelyhearts, Sick-of-it-all has no name except the abstract quality. People without identity are abstract, stylized, grotesque. It is interesting that Sick-of-it-all is a woman—Miss Lonelyhearts identifies more with women than with men—and that her problems revolve around sex and religion.[4] She has had seven children in twelve years; her kidneys hurt her. Her religion forbids the abortion of her present pregnancy. Sex and religion, instead of helping her, make her more "sick-of-it-all." Miss Lonelyhearts cannot tell her what to do—he throws her letter away and lights a cigarette. Nor can he advise "Desperate" who, like Sick-of-it-all, is feminine. Her "terrible bad fate" is also associated with physical pain: She was born without a nose! She is unable to find someone who can love her in spite of her condition. "Desperate" is informed by her Papa that she suffers because of her sins in the other world (or his sins in the present one). Her letter ends with one question which surely plagues Miss Lonelyhearts: "Ought I commit suicide?" Miss Lonelyhearts repeats his ritualistic act—he lights another cigarette after his first one "refused to draw." West's repetition of the cigarette lighting may be symbolic. Can he mean that we need more light (a traditional symbol)? Does he imply that only cigarettes, not religion, burn?

The third letter is, superficially, different from the other two. "Harold S." is more of a person than the other two; he is writing for his sister. His problem—or, rather, his sister's—is again sexual: she has been molested. Harold is tormented because he wants to tell someone of her plight. It is appropriate that Miss

Lonelyhearts does not light any more cigarettes—he is at the end of the line. He stops reading and calls upon Christ as the answer. Christ is as imperfect as the cigarettes because he is soon compared to a business and a joke (Shrike's particular one). Miss Lonelyhearts turns to the typewriter as the final solution. He is on his own; he must be his own Christ.

Only now does West give his physical description. (The metaphysical precedes or determines the physical —as in *The Dream Life of Balso Snell*.) We are informed that he has cheap clothes with "too much style" (another paradox); a "high and narrow forehead; a "long and fleshless" nose; and a "bony" chin "cleft like a hoof." The description omits his entire body—as he himself would like to do!—and persuades us that he is so ascetic as to be ghostlike or nonsubstantial. It matches his personal name (or lack of one). The "hoof" bothers us. Not only does it seem "displaced"—a chin as hoof?—it also makes us think of him as satanic. The paradoxes mount.

The chapter ends with Miss Lonelyhearts' advice (or sermon). Silence. He writes less than a dozen words —West stresses the quantity rather than the quality— before Shrike leans over his shoulder. Instead of allowing the columnist to write the same old stuff, he censors him. (He is the castrating father who always cuts.) He writes a sermon on art: *"Art is a Way Out."* Create or appreciate. Go on from there. Shrike's answer is one that was rejected (ambivalently) in *The Dream Life of Balso Snell*—art could not offer a way out of the body; it was dirtied by pain. The answer itself displays lack of art because it is an unredeemed cliché. It offers little help—to return to the key word.

The abrupt beginning of a new chapter startles us. (But, as we learn, this abruptness is part of West's technique.) Although critics have pointed to the comic-book effect of captions, to strips of action, they have, for the most part, neglected the cutting effect. It is as if Shrike edits severely—he knifes Miss Lonelyhearts'

thoughts. We move to Miss Lonelyhearts as spiritual
guide (who offers little help) to Miss Lonelyhearts as
parishioner. "Miss Lonelyhearts and the dead pan" is
the title. There is another pun—the dead pan refers to
the ironic speeches of Shrike (given at length here) and
to the absence of Pan-like fertility.[5]

Miss Lonelyhearts quits work—a spiritual guide's
work is never done!—and walks in the park. Nature is
as grotesque and unpleasant as the human body. The
air, we are told, smells as though it had been "artificially
heated." The shade is "heavy." There are no signs of
spring. Nature is, therefore, wasteland; it is dead, artificial, or inactive.[6] Perhaps the only activity lies in the
"few green spikes" torturing through the "exhausted
dirt." The spikes (especially with the word *torture*) are
brutal and phallic. They are linked to the lamppost
which gives off a shadow that pierces Miss Lonelyhearts
"like a spear." Note the associations—spikes, torture,
spear, pierce (the latter two words rhyme internally).[7]
Nature is frightening because it is both dead and alive,
exhausted and piercing. There is no happy medium, no
point of rest between opposing qualities. Miss Lonelyhearts does not want to stop in the park (as sanctuary),
but he does sit for a few minutes.

He thinks of refreshment. Water is fertile; it can help
this wasteland flower once more. Perhaps his correspondents (a pun is intended!) will "water the soil with
their tears." The flowers which would come up would
probably smell "of feet." Miss Lonelyhearts moves from
water (finally noncreative or dirty in his thoughts) to
stones.[8] He makes believe that he is Shrike—the two
continually change identities or merge in their thoughts
—and delivers a sermon on stones. They are symbolic
of rigidity, infertility, static reality, and the hard church.
They are within his gut. Miss Lonelyhearts wants to
throw them, maybe to strike back at the sky. But as
Beagle Darwin has noted, there are no objects to hit—
we are informed that the sky holds "no angels, flaming
crosses, olive-bearing doves, wheels within wheels."

Only a newspaper flies in the air—the newspaper is all there is.

The speakeasy is another possible sanctuary. It is the church in which Miss Lonelyhearts and his brothers try to find "holy water." The water is usually dirty— we see the "warm mud of alcoholic gloom." Shrike appears—he is, of course, never really out of Miss Lonelyhearts' mind—to deliver another sermon, despite being told to shut up "for Christ's sake." (Such expressions occur regularly in the novel. West uses them in an almost sacramental way.)

His sermon is hedonistic. He tells Miss Lonelyhearts to "forget the crucifixion" and remember the renaissance (alcoholic clergy, beautiful women). Ironically, he remains fixed in his facial expression—the "dead pan"— and he thus becomes associated with stones. When he mentions women, he is less interested in their sexual vitality than in his own dead grayness. He is closer to Christ than to Pan. Although he pats the rump of Miss Farkis (note the pun), he thinks more of religion than of her charms.

Shrike's real text for the day is a clipping from the newspaper. (Again the newspaper functions as a bible.) The clipping describes an adding machine which will be used to offer numbered prayers for a condemned man. Why does West empty the weird machine? Perhaps he is equating numbers and words. Both the machine and the letters written by Miss Lonelyhearts are programmed (and stonelike); [9] they cannot save others. They remain abstract and universal, not concrete.

After Shrike, Miss Farkis, and Miss Lonelyhearts— the first of the perverse trinities in the novel—find seats inside one of the booths, Shrike continues his sermon. It is a seduction speech for his partners. It mixes religion and sex. Shrike begins by claiming that he is a great saint because he can walk on his "own water." Holy water becomes urine. (Again water is impure.) He compares Christ's wounds to "a miraculous purse" (in a Freudian way) and moves quickly to the holes in the body. He repeats the holy obsessions of Balso Snell. The body is grotesquely viewed as a lush, "ripe" jungle —the intestines are "golden," the organs are "over-ripe." It is as if the wasteland symbol is linked with excess fertility—both wastes and "tropical growths" are unnatural. Shrike pictures the soul as a bird flying in the jungle-body. How to capture the bird? Religions use various devices, but they want only to trap the bird and stuff it. Shrike wants the bird to live. He is, however, less interested in the bird than in the body. He caresses Miss Farkis as he speaks. When he finishes the sermon, he buries "his triangular face like the blade of a hatchet in her neck." The sentence gives the lie to his sermon. He cannot allow the bird (or the body) to live—he must cut it. He kills for the sake of his unnatural religion. He acts out his name.

In the next chapter Miss Lonelyhearts is in another sanctuary—his home. The room is full of shadows—like the shadow of the lamppost in the park or the alcoholic gloom of Delehantys. It resembles a "steel engraving." (The steel reminds us of stone; the engraving of burial.) The only decoration is a "ivory Christ" nailed to the wall with "large spikes," but the figure does not writhe. It is fixed and stonelike.

Miss Lonelyhearts reads a chapter in *The Brothers Karamazov*. (Dostoevsky is again used as a source by West. Unlike *The Dream Life of Balso Snell*, which used "the underground man" and Raskolnikov, this novel contains the loving, Christian characters.) [10] The passage quotes Father Zossima's sermon on Love: "Love the animals, love the plants, love everything. If you love everything, you will perceive the divine mystery in things." It is an interesting contrast to the previous texts—Shrike's sermon, the newspaper clippings, and the letters from readers seeking spiritual guidance—because it assumes that Love is all-embracing. Miss Lonelyhearts regards it as excellent advice, but he realizes that he cannot follow it. His vocation is different and ambivalent. He remembers that "as a boy in his father's church," he had discovered Christ (at least the name), but had never allowed him to come alive. Because he associates Father Zossima and his own father as spiritual guides—they are replaced by Shrike as castrating father—he makes his religious conflict psychosexual.[11] "The Christ business" is colored. He cannot separate Christ from his boyish misunderstandings and tensions.

The point is especially clear in the rest of this chapter. The reality of the Dostoevsky passage, of the Christ figure on the wall, and of his present vocation, changes swiftly. Dreams break through his consciousness. Miss Lonelyhearts thinks of the Christ "thing" as "hysteria, a snake whose scales are tiny mirrors in which the dead world takes on a semblance of life." Religion becomes hysteria—the Father becomes feminine. The matter is even more perverse. Christ is viewed as a snake (Satan), a pleasing illusion of life. The mirrors suggest narcissistic involvement. Miss Lonelyhearts is ambivalent toward Christ (pictured as good and evil, masculine and feminine, real and unreal) largely as a result of his own uneasy relationship with self-image. Indeed, Christ is his self-image. Thus he must close his eyes; he cannot face the snake in his own brain.

But sleep presents more problems (or aspects of the same one). He sees himself as a magician on the stage of a crowded theater. He does tricks with doorknobs; the doorknobs bleed, flower, and speak. He tries to lead the audience in prayer but he echoes Shrike. He mocks his own words. The symbols are important here. Miss Lonelyhearts wants to be a magician; he wants to transform himself (and the audience) as well as the doorknobs. He resembles the performers—John Gilson, Beagle Darwin, Balso Snell—in the first novel but like them he is an unsuccessful, frustrated artist. He hates the others because they are mirrors—remember Christ as snake and mirror!—of his own inadequacies. Perhaps he sees all people as doorknobs; in an earlier paragraph he regards the world as doorknobs. Why doorknobs? He is wooden (or metallic or stonelike); he is outside of things; he is feminine (rounded). The door-knob is a dead circle—to use another recurring metaphor of *Balso Snell*. Miss Lonelyhearts again becomes Shrike —it is as if he is the editor's dummy, speaking in an unnatural voice. Instead of merging with the audience, he merges with Shrike. He gives himself and loses whatever identity he has.

"The scene of the dream changed." This sentence is a clue to the novel. Miss Lonelyhearts has one dream, but he views it in different surroundings. His dream —or, better yet, obsession—changes within fixed limits. (Another similarity to *Balso Snell*.) There is tension between movement and stasis not only within this chapter of dreams but within the entire novels. Scenes change; dreams do not. People act; their identities remain.

Miss Lonelyhearts dreams that he is in a college dormitory. He has been arguing religious matters with two friends. (We have another unholy trinity.) They decide to get some whisky. They wander (after buying a jug of applejack) to an open field in which they find a lamb. They parade the lamb in the marketplace. They have a ritual—Miss Lonelyhearts is elected priest—and they try to slaughter it. But the knife cannot cut through the "matted wool." They flee. Only later does Miss Lonelyhearts return to kill the lamb, crushing its head with a stone. The dream (and the chapter) ends with flies buzzing around the "bloody altar flowers."

Miss Lonelyhearts presents himself in the dream as an ineffectual priest. (In the earlier dream he was an ineffective magician.) He is ineffectual except for drunken violence—because he wants to love and destroy himself. He is the lamb—as he is the audience! His ritual of sacrifice is a crazy attempt at creative suicide. He kills himself in order to prove his existence. (*The Possessed* by Dostoevsky comes to mind.) The ritual fails apparently—we don't see his transformation as West abruptly cuts out his reactions to the dream. Only the act of violence remains.

Symbols recur. Nature is associated with death—as

in the "bloody altar flowers." The altar (is West punning on alter?) is presented as a rock. Stone is used to kill the lamb. By linking the altar—religious ceremony—to stone, Miss Lonelyhearts condemns it. It becomes an image of his own stonelike qualities. It is, of course, easy to see the sexual knife. Miss Lonelyhearts cannot use the knife because he wants to be cut (as he is pierced in the preceding chapter by the shadow of the lamppost). He wants to bleed by someone else's—Christ's? Shrike's?—hand. Then he will be redeemed.

After Miss Lonelyhearts "awakes"—it is difficult in the novel to define precisely the waking life—he walks around his room. He puts things in order. The act is symbolic—he is so afraid of his own disorder that he must limit and stabilize external objects. His violence gives way to compulsive design. He is another of our American heroes—like Ahab, Thomas Sutpen, and Nick Adams—who rigidifies existence; and like his spiritual brothers, he is unsuccessful. The inanimate world—not to mention the animate one—refuses to be balanced. It rebels. Pencil points break; collar buttons disappear; and the clock defeats him. The situation is even more desperate outside the room. People hurry past in a nonpatterned way. Their raw shouts erupt. Chaos is "multiple." Miss Lonelyhearts is a would-be "artist of the balanced"—to change Hawthorne's title slightly—but he cannot shape chaos. His attempts demonstrate his inflexible, nonorganic craftmanship. Although critics have discussed his benevolent efforts to fix people's lives, they have not completely viewed him as a mechanized artist.[12] He is another Balso Snell, attempting to get out of this world by searching for the proper strange form. Both use magical thinking as they perform (or are performed by) their tasks.

Miss Lonelyhearts also has Betty, a muse. She represents power and order. She straightens his tie: "And he had once thought that if her world were larger, were *the* world, she might order it finally as the objects on her dressing table." Betty, interestingly enough, lives on the other side of the city. She does not belong here. Despite her roundness and smoothness, she lacks sub- stance—she possesses even less character than he and his correspondents. It is no wonder that she is continu- ally criticized as she is courted. The "fat thumb" of his feelings gets in the way of real communication between them. Betty as "Buddha" irritates him as much, if not more than, the Christ.

When they sit on the couch, Miss Lonelyhearts gets jittery. He cannot remain still—perhaps stillness or bliss reminds him of death. He looks for her breast; he wants to wear her nipple in his buttonhole. He hopes by such serious clowning to startle her. She responds by asking: "Are you sick?" Sickness is the easy word; it does not completely fit Miss Lonelyhearts who suffers from a holy illness—a "Christ complex." Thus he is annoyed by her simplistic, maternal advice—even more so than by Shrike's raging sermons. He is torn, as it were, by his responses to Mother (Betty and the other women we meet later) and Father (Shrike, Christ). He dangles, not knowing where to turn.

Miss Lonelyhearts falls back on performance. He claims that he is just kidding; he doesn't mean anything. Again we have the split between performer and audience (which echoes child and parent, religionist and deity). There is mutual hate as well as attraction. The impor- tant word is "split." Although both sides (or forces) share similarities, they are, finally, in different worlds. They are alone. The chapter ends with Betty feeling "lousy" and crying to Miss Lonelyhearts: "Go away. Please go away." After an unusual dialogue—unusual in the sense that until now the novel has stressed the individual speech of Shrike or Miss Lonelyhearts—we find the desire for silence. The love talk is as destructive as self-centered preaching—probably more so, according to West!

Miss Lonelyhearts finds himself in the street (after the chapter ends suddenly) and feels as though his heart is a bomb (a violent stone?). He decides to return to the speakeasy, his other sanctuary. (Does speakeasy seem especially appropriate here? He wants a silent place, away from the words of Betty, Dostoevsky, Shrike, and his own letters.) There he listens to dirty stories about gang rape. The two stories involve female writers who are assaulted by "mugs." (They echo the violence Balso Snell displays toward the playgoers.) The reason for the stories is obscure. Although Miss Lonelyhearts thinks they destroy the cult of literary beauty—the value of art—he needs such easy explanation to comfort him. He is really less interested in the limitations of art than in revenge against women. He does not trust their motives, viewing them as false guides. He fears Betty, Mrs. Shrike (whom we shall soon meet) because they seem more powerful than he. In an analogous way he wants his Christ to fight against Mary—to be his own mother. Throughout the novel redemption and rebellion are married.

The men at the bar talk about Miss Lonelyhearts. They condemn his literary approach to religion—they see it in the same way Beagle Darwin regards literary suicide—and maintain that a "genuine religious experience" on his part would be personal and meaningless. They equate epiphany and case history. In this respect they echo West.

Miss Lonelyhearts remembers an incident of his childhood (after forgetting that his heart is a bomb). He has been waiting with his sister for their father to return from church. He was killing time—"the pause between playing and eating"—by playing a Mozart piece. His sister danced: "Square replacing oblong and being replaced by circle." He was happy.

The incident, not usually mentioned by critics, is important; it is a "religious experience." Miss Lonelyhearts discovers order in childhood—dancing and music are married (as are circle, square, and oblong in the dance pattern). The order extends to his relationship with his younger sister. They respond to each other; they make an Eden at home—away from the adults. It is interesting to note that the father is distant and the mother dead. Such absence heightens their "incestuous" peace. Miss Lonelyhearts' "religious experience" is, therefore, linked to childhood happiness. He will never repeat it—except when the proper psychological circumstances recur.

Miss Lonelyhearts cannot remain in his childhood reverie. He accidently collides with a beer-drinker, who punches him in the mouth. The adults always threaten! He gets angry at Christ, children dancing, himself. He thinks of asking Shrike to transfer him to the sports department (which would satisfy his "rage for order"?). He leaves the speakeasy with Ned Gates, another journalist.

In the park they enter a comfort station to warm up. An old man sits on one of the toilets. They taunt him, making believe that they will attack him and, later, that they (as scientists) will explore the sources of his "perversion." Miss Lonelyhearts becomes more and more involved in the role playing. Finally he twists the old man's arm, and he feels that he is twisting the arm of all the "sick and miserable, broken and betrayed, inarticulate and impotent."

The scene is dreamlike not only because of the dark, snow-filled, and isolated park in which they find themselves but because of the rapid and extreme reactions. The comfort station is an unnatural sanctuary; it is decidedly uncomfortable—more so than the speakeasy. Who is the old man? He is on one level of meaning, the representative of all the letter writers, the "broken bastards." He is as weak and confused as they are. He is also the paternal symbol. By striking out at him, Miss Lonelyhearts rebels against his own father. The questions about "homosexualistic tendencies" are especially significant. If he can prove "scientifically" that the old man (the father) is a "fag," he can stand alone. He can be his own father—without the need for others. Miss Lonelyhearts cannot admit marriage and/or reproduction into his consciousness. He wants a perfect world (the one he shared with his sister in childhood) in which old men and women do not interfere. Furthermore, Miss Lonelyhearts identifies the old man as a kind of religious figure—a priest, if you will. He must see him as ineffective and stupid—such a vision will make him less guilty about rebellion. Perhaps this is why he agrees to the adjective "clean." He wants to wipe his own slate clean but in doing so, he must remove the "dirty," mixed feelings of others. Cleanliness is abstract violence.

The entire scene is echoed when Miss Lonelyhearts thinks of a small frog. He steps on it accidentally. His pity turns to rage as its suffering becomes "real to his senses." He beats it frantically.

"Miss Lonelyhearts and Mrs. Shrike," the next chapter, begins with Miss Lonelyhearts lying on his bed fully dressed. His room; his thoughts; his pain—all are said to revolve like wheels. The wheel image reinforces the circularity and repetitiveness of his life—it suggests that he goes in circles, never really progressing in his quest except in an ironic, retrograde way. His childhood is the center of the circle.

When Miss Lonelyhearts gets up—it will be more difficult for him to do so as the novel develops—he takes a bath. His body feels good, but his heart remains a "congealed lump of icy fat." The fat is related to stone; it also cannot grow. "Icy" makes it even more unhealthy and rigid. (Perhaps the icy quality should make us remember his "cold and sodden" anger in the preceding chapter.) Nevertheless he is able to gain enough energy to leave his room. Again he walks in the park; soon, growing tired, he slumps on a bench. (How often he returns to the same places—Delehanty's, the park, the room!) He gazes at the obelisk.

It is a "stone shaft" which "casts a long, rigid shadow." He is that stone—a monument to his private religion—and he casts, as well as contains, the shadow. He wants rigidity. But at the same time, he is "jerky," erratic, and afraid of his "power"—he sees the monument's shadow "lengthening in rapid jerks." The phallic quality is especially clear when West makes the monument seem "red and swollen in the dying sun, as though it were about to spout a load of granite seed." Reproduction of granite is grotesque, when it is associated with dying sun—a pun on son—it becomes even more so. Can we say that Miss Lonelyhearts is potent only with stones?

He flees from the obelisk (another flight!), hoping to find a woman. A woman is a "thing" for his momentary pleasure—for relaxing the muscles. She does not exist as a person. We have seen him with Betty the Buddha (a blank object). Now we see him with Mary Shrike (at first in his reverie). She is a sexual thing—at least up to a point—and she is described in terms of odors, grunts, hollows. She resembles the naked girl in the poster at Delehanty's: her nipples dominate the scene. Miss Lonelyhearts wants to be nursed; he apparently longs for the mother (Mary, no less!) he never knew well. But Mrs. Shrike frustrates him. She is not completely available. Maybe he admires her for this very reason?

Miss Lonelyhearts arrives at the Shrike's apartment. (He is, finally, in another setting.) Shrike greets him with the word *homebreaker* and taunts him with accusations. He, of course, does not care about his wife's infidelity, because he is secretly fond of him. The men use Mary to get at each other. Shrike can exert power; Miss Lonelyhearts can feel guilty. The woman, perhaps, is more powerful than they. She is a fighter—"sleeping with her is like sleeping with a knife in one's groin." [19] She is thus equated with the phallic knife. It is almost as if she resembles the monument in the park. Her shadow dominates her sexual partners. And they like this situation! "It's Mary who does the beating."

Miss Lonelyhearts and Mrs. Shrike—an odd couple! —go to El Gaucho, a romantic nightclub. It is a dream palace (like the speakeasy, the church, the newspaper office) which caters to the desperate longings of people who write to Miss Lonelyhearts for help.[14] It is all illusion—outlandish costumes, exotic foods—and the fakery irritates him because he cannot yield to it. He sees clearly; he cannot be nourished by such humble dreams of glory. (The breast is mentioned again.)

Miss Lonelyhearts thinks of his "sickness." He cannot let go. He drowns as a "cold wave" of his readers crashes over the illusions. Reality weakens him.[15] He asks for help, wanting to see Mary's medal (which covers her breast). But before he does, she tells him about her mother's painful illness. Miss Lonelyhearts stops listening. He realizes that "parents are also part of the business of dreams." People want to talk about something poetic—something besides clothing, business, and sex—and they dramatize their backgrounds. But he stops short! He does not understand that his own dreams of religious salvation and glory are rooted in his childhood—in his priestly father (and "missing" mother). At last he returns to Mary and reads the medal (or amulet?). She was awarded the medal for first place in the 100-yard dash!

They leave the club and continue their love-making in the cab. He vents his anger at her (and the world) by caressing her body methodically and violently. His "icyness" remains. Although "a spark [flares] in his groin" at the door of her apartment, she keeps talking, trying to cool the situation. She mentions her mother's illness, her father's mistreatment. She allows him to undress her, but she leaves unscathed. The door opens. Shrike, without pajama bottoms, gazes out. He is ready for another victory.

Miss Lonelyhearts is at his desk as the next chapter opens. The coldness of the city room is mentioned, but he thinks of a "desert" which contains "rust and body dirt." It is surrounded by posters describing the crazy events of the day. The desert expands until it includes "all the news fit to print." He is startled to find Gold-smith—an interesting name contrasted with the rust and stone—handing him a letter from another "admirer."

The letter—it is the fourth that we have read so far—is from Fay Doyle. It is significant that her name is mentioned; she is not merely an abstraction like "Desperate." She asks to meet Miss Lonelyhearts; she wants more than an easy answer in the paper. She hopes for personal response. She disturbs him so much that he throws the letter into the wastepaper basket.

He returns to his column [16]—another pun, suggesting rigid, stonelike behavior?—pounding out clichés about joy-giving senses, sweet-smelling pines, foam-decked sea. But he runs out of material. He ends with " 'Life is. . . .' " He reaches for the discarded letter, thinking of it as a pink tent (another shelter image) set over the desert he had visualized before. The paper becomes rich and flesh-colored. Mrs. Doyle fuses with the paper—she is "a tent, hair-covered and veined"—and he fuses with her, making her "flesh tent" flower. Although he imagines such fertility, he remains "cold and dry as a polished bone."

Miss Lonelyhearts is such a complete failure that he surrenders to the telephone. He calls Mrs. Doyle from a booth "covered with obscene drawings." The booth is another ironic sanctuary—here he "confesses" his incompleteness which is linked to "disembodied genitals" on the wall. The adjective "disembodied," coupled with the unseen Mrs. Doyle, suggests that he is tempted now to get out of his skin—that enclosure which restricts his freedom of movement. He seeks to transcend the body. He longs to go on a "field trip" (to use the title of the chapter).

Miss Lonelyhearts arranges to meet Mrs. Doyle in the park. Of course, he sits near the obelisk. He is less interested in this talisman than in the sky. The sky is pictured as a tent (another shelter—of divinity?), but this tent is "ill-stretched." Not only does "ill-stretched" convey the lack of proper order in the universe (continuing his obsession with order), but it becomes an image of his own personality. He has been stretched by his illness. The words are two-sided. Is the sky really

"ill-stretched" or does it mirror his illness? Such ambi-
guity is important. We are getting the reality through
his consciousness—thus we are constantly unsure of
West's position. It is safe, however, to believe that at
least some of their metaphors are married. West and
Miss Lonelyhearts share patterns of perception.

Miss Lonelyhearts turns from the sky to the sky-
scrapers. He regards them as stones which display
peculiar American energy. The energy has been dissi-
pated. Perhaps by mentioning the Egyptians, he means
to imply that the stones are our tombs. They are built
to satisfy perverse religion.

Mrs. Doyle enters the park. She is even more grotesque than the other characters we have met. The first
adjective we are offered is "big," but it is immediately
modified: her legs are like "Indian clubs"; her breasts
are like "balloons." She resembles a "police captain." [17]
Mrs. Doyle is pictured as an overwhelming, powerful
force—it is difficult to call her a woman!—which can
ride over things in her way. It is significant that Miss
Lonelyhearts passively follows her. She will lead him to
salvation—to death of his personality. Her "massive"
hams are "like two enormous grindstones"—they will
pulverise him, helping him achieve the destruction he
has secretly courted.

In Miss Lonelyhearts' apartment they sit on the bed.
She pursues him—he gets a "strange pleasure" in this
reversal of roles. She kisses his mouth; undresses, making
"sea-sounds." The sea-image continues as they make
love, but the more we see of the image, the more violent
it becomes. We suddenly realize that we have moved
again from one extreme to the other—from the wasteland (and stone) to the whirlwind. Nature is unnatural.
Miss Lonelyhearts is an "exhausted swimmer leaving the
surf." He is more tired than before.

The roles are reversed once more. Mrs. Doyle plays
the passive role. She is "ashamed" of herself; she confesses to him. She says that her husband is "all dried
up"—the wasteland enters!—and hasn't satisfied her

for years. He is crippled. They were married because he agreed to look after her and her child (born out of wedlock). Mr. Doyle is a "queer guy," his wife continues, and he always makes believe that he is the father. When the girl objects, he hits her. He moves easily from passivity to violence. He is even now (before we meet him in person) a mirror of Miss Lonelyhearts— especially in his queer shifts of emotion; his desire to be the spiritual father of the world; and in his crippled ways.

Miss Lonelyhearts hears the entire confession and begins to offer clichés. He claims that "your husband probably loves you and the kid." He calls her "pretty." These clichés do not hide his fear. We are not told the reasons for his fear—he himself does not know why— but we can assume that he wants to avoid complications. But the Doyle family is complex. He "loves" both. He enjoys being dragged down by Mrs. Doyle and seeing himself as Mr. Doyle. He must eventually choose one— the decision will not be easy because he will have to make it on the basis of his childhood desires and fears. For the time being he sleeps, rewarded with a kiss by Mrs. Doyle, his big mother.

He sleeps so well that he falls into the "dismal swamp" of the following chapter. His imagination, however, works steadily. He finds himself in a pawnshop full of various "paraphernalia of suffering": guns, mandolins, rings. The objects are human at times: a horn, for example, "grunted with pain." (Remember "grunt" from the encounter with Mrs. Doyle.) They force us to recognize that in the grotesque world of Miss Lonelyhearts, people and objects change places.[18] He is less a person than a stone, shadow, or would-be obelisk; Mrs. Shrike is a breast or medal; Mrs. Doyle is a balloon. Perhaps they are abstractions—like the names of the correspondents—because they have surrendered to the objects around them. Miss Lonelyhearts, indeed, wants to see Christ reborn—to jump out from the cross which inhibits his vitality.

In the pawnshop (another ironic sanctuary?) Miss Lonelyhearts philosophizes. He generalizes: "Man has a tropism for order." His generalization is, of course, based on his own (not-so-special?) case. It is modified by the concreteness of "Mandolins are tuned GDAE." (West, as we know, hates pedantic theory; he always tries to bring ideas down to earth.) When we remember his childhood music-playing, we make a useful connection. Order and music (art in general) go together.

Opposed to such order "in the battle of the centuries" is entropy. The physical world (including the body so disliked by all of West's heroes) strives for disorder. Even mandolins seek to "get out of tune." The generalization is a bit simple-minded—what causes the tropisms?—but it is perfectly suitable in the novel's context. It reinforces the dynamic, stylized forces at work.

Miss Lonelyhearts wants to shape things. He yearns for his own order. He builds a man out of junk—a double of sorts. First he forms the phallus out of watches and rubber boots; then a heart of umbrellas. It is interesting that he wants the phallus and the heart (in that sequence!): he is dissatisfied with his own equipment. Miss Lonelyhearts is not a master builder; unable to build a man, he begins to make a "gigantic cross." The cross grows in size (as it has through the novel) until it exhausts him. He staggers, loaded down with "marine refuse." He cannot control the Christ business because he regards it as a cross, not as a human and/or superhuman task. Faith is viewed objectively. Why does Miss Lonelyhearts link the cross to marine refuse? Does he see Mrs. Doyle (pictured previously in sea-terms) as another savior? Has he confused sexual and religious salvation? Such questions heighten the effect.

When Betty arrives to take care of him, she walks gently into the room with her arms full of bundles. (The bundles remind us of the cross in the dream.) She offers hot soup, joining Mrs. Doyle as mother-confessor. Although he is annoyed by her "wide-eyed little mother act," he is too tired to say anything. He simply makes apologies. Betty, in turn, gives advice which, like his columns, goes against the grain of reality: Work in an advertising agency! Forget the letters!

How can Miss Lonelyhearts answer her? He tries to start at the beginning. At first his job was a joke, but it slowly began to get away from him. He couldn't enjoy the comedy—suffering (of the letter-writers and letter-readers) got in the way. He became the victim of the joke. (Like the performers in *The Dream Life of Balso Snell*, he was caught in his own mask—he married it.) [19] His passivity won.

After Betty tells him about the joy of country living —she advises him to live there!—she leaves without saying good-by. Shrike rushes into the room. (It seems as if they, like Mrs. Doyle, need to see him at home. They make their own "field trips.") He is in rare form —he is "unescapable." He offers a lengthy sermon on escapism—it is, perhaps, the climactic point of the novel; it forces Miss Lonelyhearts to realize that he cannot run away from his troubles.

Shrike cites the virtues of country life, beginning where Betty stopped. He mixes poetry and cliché so artfully that there are moments in which we feel that he is in love with nature before he finally destroys it. He mentions the crowded subway, the getting and spending of business. Then he moves in a typically Romantic way to the farm—except that he describes the horse's "moist behind." Pine needles and dung mix. Shrike dramatically stops, asking Miss Lonelyhearts whether he agrees with the soil as answer. There is no reply. Silence is the answer to dull and laborious escape.

Shrike extends country life to the South Seas. Here too is no escape. He describes the breasts and belly of a slim young maiden, the golden brown of Miss Lonelyhearts. His words are lush, over-ripe (like the clichéd picture they describe). They laugh at themselves as when they concentrate upon "silvery moon" or "blue lagoon." Their rhymes call attention to easy stupidity. Thus when Shrike comes to the "society girl" and the "secret of happiness," we are again prepared for Miss Lonelyhearts' silence.

But Shrike (and West) cannot stop. He must continue to rant. He moves now to Hedonism as escape (which includes country life and South Seas?). The body is a pleasure machine: golf, booze, and even Proust are condemned. One last party before death is described. The caviar, blackberries, and coffee cannot hide Miss Lonelyhearts' despair as he proclaims (according to Shrike): "Don't squawk." Silence once more!

Shrike has been building his sermon in such a way as to tempt Miss Lonelyhearts progressively. Now he is ready for Art as an escape. He echoes *The Dream Life of Balso Snell* (more so than in his previous comments). He offers the spiritual food of Bach, Brahms, and Beethoven. (The 3 B's heighten the cliché-effect). It is interesting to note that Shrike stresses passive nourishment. He does not see himself or Miss Lonelyhearts (for they are "married") as an active, creative participant. Art is like breast-feeding. Shrike doesn't even wait for a silent answer; he moves quickly to suicide and drugs.

The goal of his sermon is religion. Shrike admits that "we are not men who swallow camels only to strain at stools." The spiritual food turns into excrement—as in Balso Snell's dreams. He proclaims the "church as our only hope," but he immediately undercuts this hope by describing Christ as Dentist—the "Preventer of Decay." Why the dental work? West apparently suggests that Christ can prevent our decay caused by improper dieting. He can fix things. But Christ is not seen as proper, wholesome nourishment. Shrike's comparison is so ironic that it destroys the hope mentioned in the first part of the same sentence.

He continues, dictating a letter to "Miss Lonelyhearts of Miss Lonelyhearts"—that is, Christ. The repetition of names is important; it leads later to Miss Lonelyhearts' marriage with himself as Christ. Now the columnist is fully identified as "a regular subscriber," as another correspondent. Shrike gives us Miss Lonely-hearts' biography—an ironic saint's life—but he also takes the other's role. He writes a kind of autobiography. He uses clichés, but they are redeemed, as it were, because we see that they are earned. Life is a "desert" echoes the wasteland imagery. The "walls of my citadel" reinforces the sanctuary (or "perilous chapel"—to follow the wasteland image). "I feel like hell" accurately captures the spiritual (and physical) condition. Shrike mutilates the clichés (he preys on them) by punning on "Saviour" and the "saviour" of salt. Both are insufficient in adding flavor to life. He asks in advance for a quick reply, knowing he will not get one and will, therefore, remain a regular subscriber.

The biographical letter—which is, in effect, a micro-cosm of the novel itself—ends. There is complete silence. Neither Shrike nor Miss Lonelyhearts says any-thing.[20] Their final hopes have fled.

The next chapter "Miss Lonelyhearts in the Country," begins slowly in contrast to the accelerating speed of Shrike's sermon. Miss Lonelyhearts continues to stay in bed and to nourish himself on soup and chicken. His passivity grows as he disregards his present sickness. He tries to tell Betty about Christ and the letters, but he does not get far. She instructs him not to think about such horrible things. She remains the good mother (un-like Mrs. Doyle or Mrs. Shrike) not wanting her son to get overly excited.

As the chapter progresses, we notice that her role is stressed. She takes over for the time being. She gives him a walk in the zoo, pointing out the "curative power of animals": "she seemed to think that it must steady him to look at a buffalo." She has a plan. She will take him to her aunt's farm in Connecticut—she was born there—and they will camp in the house (enjoying the pleasures he has already given up).

Betty is too silly and weak to remain the all-knowing (and all-comforting) mother. She becomes an "excited child" as they get closer to trees and grass. The farm is

musty smelling, but she does not complain because it is
not a "human smell." The detail is important. She
hates the stink of humanity; she is so afraid of it that
she must disguise or forget it. Miss Lonelyhearts cannot—he complains. But he is swayed momentarily. He
joins in the game they play. He is a natural child again.
(Perhaps he thinks of her as his younger sister; they
play "house" in the absence of parents.) He cleans the
old mattress—like his moldy thoughts? He eats simple
food.

The characteristic ironies are missing as West describes the two of them. He makes us believe that
nature is not a complete wasteland. The flies, the lily
pads, the crickets, and the stars—nothing disturbs the
"still point." Peace reigns in the country sanctuary. But
it cannot last. The tensions begin to mount. A villager
claims the "yids" kill deer. The "funereal hush" dominates "rotten leaves, gray and white fungi. . . ." It
gets unpleasantly hot. Betty is unable to sit still; she
compulsively works around the house. Even her breasts
—again West obsessively describes breasts!—become
somewhat unpleasant: "they were like pink-tipped
thumbs." (The "fat thumb" was used in an earlier
chapter to describe Miss Lonelyhearts' inability to
communicate.) The thrush sings; its sound resembles
that of a "flute choked with saliva." The leaves are "an
army of little metal shields" as the sun beats down upon
them.[21]

The "childishly sexual" nature of their field trip is
emphasized in the last paragraph. Miss Lonelyhearts
vaults the porch rail—his most active movements of
the novel so far!—and runs to kiss Betty. He smells "a
mixture of sweat, soap and crushed grass" as they lie
down. The mixture is the final result and it is decidedly
unpleasant.

They drive back to the city; the return accelerates the
foreboding. In the Bronx slums Miss Lonelyhearts
knows that he has not been cured. His complaints per-
sist. He cannot be a faker and fool to satisfy Betty.

When he sees the crowds, he is shocked. They move with "dream-like violence"—the dream of country living flees quickly!—and their mouths are torn. Individuals are noticed: a man staggers into a movie theater which is showing *Blonde Beauty*;[22] a ragged woman reads a love story magazine. The contrasts between the reality and the dream (which he has seen in his own condition) are then generalized. Miss Lonelyhearts knows that we do not have glorious dreams anymore—we dream in clichés given to us by movies or love story magazines. The Christ dream is unusual, but it is also sick. Where can the dream be purified of illness? How can he become humble?

These questions plague him so much that he goes right to bed. He vows to cleanse himself. At work the next day, he types: "Christ died for you." This message is the first he has written in a long while (and the first he has written without responding to a specific letter). But he cannot completely believe it—it slips away as do the physical details outside his window. It is raining. Perhaps West is suggesting the fertility outside (and inside)—the slow drips indicate necessary change.

Miss Lonelyhearts picks up "a bulky letter in a dirty envelope." He reads it (for the rest of the chapter). It presents a picture of a "broad-shouldered" woman who has been married to a stupid, lazy, and mad man. She writes about her steady work, her missing husband (he leaves and returns), and her desire not to have more children. The marital relationship is described at length. It is, as we would expect, sadomasochistic. She is threatened: her husband keeps under his pillow scissors, knife, stone lifter (the latter is especially interesting in the imagistic context of the novel). The pressures continue to mount. She looks under her bed and she sees his "face like the mask of a devil with only the whites of the eyes showing." She finally accepts his craziness, but she won't put him away. Her long letter concludes with the statement that she cannot tell all her woes—they "would fill a book."

The silence at the end of the chapter is particularly revealing. In the past Miss Lonelyhearts tried to offer some clichés—even during Shrike's nasty, realistic sermon, he shook his head or turned toward the wall. Now he "disappears." He cannot play the role or even laugh at it (as do the performers in *The Dream Life of Balso Snell*). He has "returned"—to use the key word of the chapter—and died.

In the following chapter Miss Lonelyhearts continues to be humble. Humility is linked "madly" with the disappearance of self. He "dodges" Betty; he fails to call her back; he gets "below self-laughter." He begins to act like Bartleby, the scrivener. He also "prefers not to."

Although he agrees to go to Delehanty's with Goldsmith, he is so humble at this point that he does not completely know where he is. His humility is tinged with illness—it is difficult, indeed, to separate the two. Shrike, who is at Delehanty's, underlines the union by suggesting that faith is health, lack of faith is illness. Does he regard himself as ill? He does not bother to answer the question—if he were able to, he would no longer be a shrike—preferring the familiar jokes. He calls Miss Lonelyhearts "brother." Of course, they are —if not doubles!

There is a change in these familiar jokes. Miss Lonelyhearts smiles at them as "the saints are supoed to have smiled at those about to martyr them." His humility is without limits. Even Shrike is slightly different—he is, if it is possible, more violent now. He laughs at his laughter, appearing to be offended: "You cannot believe, you can only laugh." How duplicitous!

After Shrike uses the word *kills*, the bartender breaks in to address Miss Lonelyhearts. He informs him that a "gent"—"gentleman" is heavy with meanings in the context—named Doyle wants to speak to him. The little cripple immediately moves closer, making "many waste motions, like those of a partially destroyed insect." "Insect" is linked to the other wasteland images (and to the animal-human ones), but the adjectival "partially destroyed" is more interesting for our purpose. Doyle is destroyed and destroyer; he combines pity and killing—thus the appearance right after Shrike's "kill." He is vulnerable, but he also makes others vulnerable. I stress these paradoxical qualities because if we agree with Shrike that Doyle is "mankind, mankind . . . ," then we must understand his ambivalent, disturbing status.

We learn more about the cripple. He inspects meters for the gas company. He is a symbolic judge—later he will evaluate the wisdom of Miss Lonelyhearts and fulfill the function of the biblical Peter (by being a rock on which the new church will be constructed). He is also the "iceman." He says: we "meter inspectors take the place of the iceman in the stories." He leers. If we remember the icy images describing Miss Lonelyhearts earlier, we can note the further doubleness of cripple and columnist. Both men are icy, stonelike, and partially destroyed. Is it reading too much into the novel to transpose insect and incest? Doyle and Miss Lonelyhearts share brotherly love. They smile at each other.

In the back room—even more of a sanctuary!—the two men stare at each other, sharing an excitement of wordless communication. This fact is significant. The novel has been dominated by newspaper print, letters asking advice, Shrike's lectures. Words have been burdensome. Now silence is pregnant with meaning. Doyle gives "birth"—the cliché I have used in my last sentence is redeemed!—to "groups of words that lived inside of him as things. . . ." But these words are jumbled and "mute."

The next paragraph is fascinating. Miss Lonelyhearts gets ready to hear Peter's confession "like a priest," with his face slightly turned." He looks more than he listens. He watches the cripple's gestures; they become poetic. There is illumination as the hands illustrate a matter with "which he was already finished, or move ahead to illustrate something he had not yet begun to talk about." [23] The disjointed play of hands grows until Doyle breaks the spell by forcing a letter upon Miss Lonelyhearts. In a way the letter is anticlimactic—it means less than his gestures.

The letter is the first written by an adult male. It is addressed to "a man and not some dopey woman." Doyle complains about his lack of advancement, his crippled condition, and his age, but his primary complaint is about extreme pain. He describes it in detail so that it (or, more specifically, his injured leg) becomes a symbol of the human condition. He wants to "no" —his misspelling is peculiarly appropriate as another pun—"what is the whole stinking business for."

Doyle's "damp hand" accidently touches Miss Lonelyhearts' hand. The columnist jerks away. Then he clasps the other's hand "with all the love he could manage." They sit silently. The hand clasp (or embrace) is the answer to the painful questions of the letter. It is beyond words—a lonely, heartfelt gesture of love.

In the next chapter, the two men (or, better yet, the two aspects of the same man) leave the speakeasy. (Speakeasy reverberates with new meaning now.) They both call on Christ. Doyle hopes that Christ will blast his wife and his crippled foot—that he will become a vengeful deity. Miss Lonelyhearts, conversely, calls on Christ as a "shape" of joy. The conflict between the two Christs is important—it prefigures the paradoxical, tense quality of final religious belief.

The men are no longer happy when they go to Doyle's apartment. Mrs. Doyle is the menacing third party. She possesses more power than either man, and she exerts it, pressing her knee against Miss Lonelyhearts. They drink highballs. Mrs. Doyle continues to touch the columnist—her husband objects, although he laughs apologetically, and he shows momentary rage. This rage disappears as he plays the dog for her, catching the newspaper in his teeth. The detail is odd. It is obvious that he is a poor animal, dependent upon his wife-owner, but why should West include the detail of the newspaper? Perhaps he wants us to remember that just as Doyle catches the newspaper, the newspaper catches him (all of the characters). It is the controlling force; it acknowledges communication between people (correspondent and columnist) at the same time that it denies close togetherness. It is paradoxically, a uniting and dividing totem.

There is another curious detail. Doyle tears open Miss Lonelyhearts' fly! [24] Although it seems likely that we are to get a sense of the latent homosexual bond between the men (as we did with Miss Lonelyhearts and the clean old man), we are not really given the reasons for Doyle's action. Is he making an advance to compete with his wife? Does he want to humiliate Miss Lonelyhearts? Is he deflating sexual attachments? These disturbing questions are not easily answered (or separated). But the gesture is in marked contrast to the earlier hand-holding; it demonstrates Doyle's unpredictable violence.

After the tableau the three return to their seats. Silence bothers them. (This is in contrast to the silence of the speakeasy.) Miss Lonelyhearts searches for a message (as he has throughout the novel); Doyle and his wife simply stare at each other. The silence becomes so empty (or full?) that they are annoyed. They scream; they have to "say something." Mrs. Doyle runs out of the room. The men then smile and hold hands once more. They are called "fairies" by her.

The message comes now. Miss Lonelyhearts realizes that he must extol the virtues of marriage and forgiveness. He speaks in clichés, using such words as "pain," "dream," "life," and "weariness." The words desperately hide the realities of the situation. They are beyond the fact. Thus they embarrass Doyle and astonish Mrs. Doyle. Even Miss Lonelyhearts knows that they are ridiculous.

He tries again. He brings in Christ, hopefully avoiding the romantic, purely humanistic words he used previously. "Christ is love," he proclaims (screams is the more accurate word). He understands, however, that

Christ is also a cliché. He tries a metaphor, hoping to go, in a primitive way beyond words to realities: "Christ is the black fruit that hangs on the crosstree." Why black fruit? Can he see Christ as newsprint—as "all the news that's fit to print"? The black fruit does not seem particularly attractive, but in a wasteland, it suffices, especially in the midst of stone or ice. West may be more subtle. Miss Lonelyhearts admits that he feels like an empty bottle because he is using Shrike's rhetoric, not his own. He himself does not know what black fruit means.

Miss Lonelyhearts sees that despite his limited vocabulary, the Doyles are kissing. For a moment he is pleased. But when he is left alone with Mrs. Doyle, who puts on a jazz orchestra, he begins to tire. The noise, the obscene gestures—these realities are more troublesome (if this is possible) than the words he uses (or abuses). He feels like an "empty bottle that is being slowly filled with warm dirty water." He is no longer "shiny and sterile." The water is fertile only in contrast to stone. When it merges with (or becomes) the "milk" of her breasts, he becomes violent. He hits her again and again, declaring his opposition to faith (her name, we remember, is Fay) in humanity. He bolts out of the house.

We are prepared to see Miss Lonelyhearts in bed after this incident—throughout the novel he alternates between "field trips" and sleeping—but we note that this time he is more desperate. He is riding his bed, seeking some promised land far away. (His voyage is a three-day affair; perhaps West plays with the idea of Christ's death.) He is calm, silent, and thirsty—the various adjectives are linked with previous images. He sleeps the sleep of the wise and the innocent. But he dreams. He sees himself as a "reclining statue" (a stone man again!) holding a stopped clock; as a guitar-player (music again!), shedding the rain with his hump. The dreams merge with his waking state (as they do in *The Dream Life of Balso Snell*) and when he climbs out of bed to answer the knocking on his door, he is unsure about his present condition. Miss Lonelyhearts' nakedness is interesting. As he approaches his "religious experience"—the novel has been moving to this end—he strips himself of various illusions. He is bare (and barren!).

A group rushes in when he opens the door. Three men hold their ground; two women shriek and leave quickly. All are drunk. Shrike dashes at Miss Lonelyhearts (as Doyle will later) because he thinks his nakedness insults the women. Probably he distrusts it for its potential power—that power which he has been fighting. The description of Shrike and Miss Lonelyhearts is significant: "Shrike dashed against him, but fell back, as a wave that dashes against an ancient rock, smooth with experience, falls back." Shrike is viewed as the active force which is defeated (for the first time!) by an ancient, unyielding obstacle. The rock of Miss Lonelyhearts is smooth with experience; it has weathered things before and it will withstand more "dashes." The irony is appealing. By becoming more stonelike, he loses his sensitivity. He powerfully loses himself. Both men are therefore defeated!

The dialogue emphasizes these tensions. Shrike tries to reassert his power, slapping him on the back. The slapping, like the previous dash, has an effect. Miss Lonelyhearts does not respond, except to pop a cracker in his mouth. (Is the cracker a wafer? Does he celebrate his own power in this inverted ritual?) Shrike gets more irritated. He needs him to play a game, assume a role, but he cannot be more than a "screaming, clumsy gull." He cannot be a shrike any longer. Miss Lonelyhearts remains solid, "perfect," and smooth. We admire his new condition while we realize that it is deathlike.

The group goes to a party in Shrike's apartment. Miss Lonelyhearts continues to be firm (and nonexistent), and when the crowd surges forward to insult him, he smiles. They slip back in a "futile curl"; the waves (related to Mrs. Doyle?) are defeated. Betty is there, "splashing" for attention. When he does not answer her, we realize the extent of his hard-earned, sick victory.

The game begins. It is the culmination of the various role-playings, performances, and spectacles we have encountered. Shrike introduces Miss Lonelyhearts to the party, claiming that he will be the spiritual guide. Of course, he is taunting him, but even as he states his cleansing, fiery power in ironic terms, he is yielding to the myth. Miss Lonelyhearts is already beginning to prevail, although his name is taken in vain.

Shrike becomes an unwilling disciple. He distributes the days' letters, reading them aloud. He makes fun of them, punning on such words as *rheum* or ridiculously allegorizing individual pain. He is the fitful sea, but his power is limited because the silence of Miss Lonelyhearts continues to triumph. Shrike builds to the word *pain* (repeated six times), and he does not even notice that the spiritual guide has left with Betty.

Announcing himself as the true disciple now that the master has disappeared, he reads another letter. It asks why Miss Lonelyhearts is a dirty skunk; it claims that he has tried to rape his wife. It is signed "Doyle." The letter jars us. It is more violent than any of the previous letters or speeches of Shrike. It has gone beyond pity into a new realm of power. How ironic! Shrike's power decreases; Doyle's increases. There will be no earthly rest for Miss Lonelyhearts!

Therefore it is appropriate that at this point Shrike eulogizes the master. He offers saint's life, as it were, drowned in clichés. He reduces uniqueness in one last attempt to prey upon him. He makes him appear to be only another pathetic man "struggling valiantly to realize a high ideal." He does not end the eulogy. He says "And so. . . ." The final moments of Miss Lonelyhearts' life are left open, but we sense that they will soon conclude violently.

Miss Lonelyhearts and Betty talk in the hall (to counterpoint the party noise). His mind, "the instrument with which he knew the rock," is touched, but he manages to keep calm. He smiles (actually grins) at her. He suggests that they have an ice-cream soda, largely as a result of acting a boy-with-girl. The fact that we have moved so quickly from Shrike, pain, Doyle's letter to a "date" heightens the black comedy of the situation.

The cuteness—unwitting, silly, and ironic—continues. Miss Lonelyhearts tries to fit into the situation, saying only what she wants to hear. He will look for a job in an advertising agency! He will remain loyal! He will love her! But at one point Betty starts crying. His "rock" is not affected—it is "oblivious to wind or rain"—as he follows her into the taxi. She is pregnant. The admission is shocking because it is the first intrusion of reality into the party atmosphere. It places her into the same category (in a less painful way) as the correspondents. It forces Miss Lonelyhearts to act. He cannot play the role of husband and father very well, but he begs her to marry him. He says all the things she expects to hear—things that go with "strawberry sodas and farms in Connecticut." (Consider that juxtaposition! Nature is made cute!) She even believes him.

The chapter ends on a rocky note. Miss Lonelyhearts does not feel. (Before he felt too much to be effective!) He smiles. He finds perfection in the complete absence of identity. When "he climbs aboard the bed again," he has passed the test. He has become as abstract as the words he employs.

West does not want us to admire Miss Lonelyhearts. He makes him feverish at the beginning of the last chapter. The fever promises "heat and mentally unmotivated violence." It is, therefore, equated with his self-destruction (which he has sought as an escape). The furnace burns everything.

When Miss Lonelyhearts fastens his eyes on the Christ, it becomes a "bright fly, spinning with quick grace on a background of blood velvet sprinkled with tiny nerve stars." The description is painstaking. Christ illuminates the room, but the brightness is shocking.

It is also violent (perhaps echoing the furnace image) because it is associated with "tiny nerve stars." Although the fly "spins," it reflects or imitates the blood of others. Christ is viewed as the reflecting mirror of violence because "it is all mental."

The room itself is "dead." (The word prepares us for the actual death later.) Things—including books—are black; they long to rise to the "bright bait" on the wall as does Miss Lonelyhearts, who is part of the room. They do rise with a "splash of music." The music alerts us again to Miss Lonelyhearts' childhood Eden with his sister and Mozart. He hopes to be one with Christ in a desperate effort to merge with "life and light" (the "life and light" he knew briefly as a child). He calls "Christ Christ!"; the shout echoes "through the innermost cells of his body." He wants to get out of his cell (the room and "the body's cage"), to fly like Christ on the wall.

Miss Lonelyhearts is clean and cool now. He "flowers." His heart becomes a "rose"—he rises as a rose; the pun is unmistakable—and presumably it is no longer lonely. He feels grace in himself and, consequently, in the room which is no longer black but rose-colored. His nerves are like small blue flowers. The various flowers are, of course, highly deceptive. West knows that we can easily respond to the prettiness and comfort of pastoral, especially after the wasteland imagery, but he tries to make us realize the futility and madness of natual thinking. The nerves as blue flowers—the description is grotesque because it is so sudden and unearned! It is a sick parody of real feeling (the feeling Miss Lonelyhearts has finally succeeded in killing).

Miss Lonelyhearts is conscious of two rhythms (his and Christ's) which now marry. He is Christ. His religious experience is upsetting because it is so closely linked with madness. (West has married two rhythms, the clinical and the religious, throughout the novel.) We cannot agree to it; we question its validity. Our acceptance is incomplete—and the fact that we (and

West) are conscious of two different rhythms (or styles of life) redeems us from the "suicide" of Miss Lonelyhearts. As he submits drafts of his "column"—his life is seen as that column!—to Christ, we understand that he now views Christ as his editor (or, better yet, co-editor). Miss Lonelyhearts is the newspaper and the reader and the writer. He is text and context. By being all things to all people, he is nothing.

The doorbell rings. Miss Lonelyhearts gets out of bed to see Doyle, slowly working his way up the stairs. He interprets the arrival as a sign—a miracle of sorts. He rushes to embrace the cripple, hoping that they will be made whole again. West uses the word *whole* in a subtle manner. It is a pun on *hole* (an opening or wound) and holy. The word joins the three meanings, suggesting that holiness is a wound. The religious experience is bloody.

We see that Doyle carries "something wrapped in a newspaper." How fitting that his weapon is hidden by the very pages of Miss Lonelyhearts' column! How fitting that it is phallic! When Miss Lonelyhearts charges the cripple, running to succor him with love, we get an inventory of names from correspondents— Sick-of-it-all, Desperate, Harold S. Both men do not really see each other; they are overshadowed, as it were, by all the hurt and pain they have encountered in their lives. They are both Christlike, carrying the cross on their shoulders.

The end is vivid. Miss Lonelyhearts and Doyle fight in the presence of Betty. (Again there is a third party.) She contributes to the confusion; her well-meaning gestures startle them. When the gun explodes finally— a complete illumination—they fall "part of the way down the stairs." They touch in death. There is no additional commentary, no need for useless words.

I have explicated *Miss Lonelyhearts* at great length. It demands close reading because it is a complex pattern of opposition and juxtaposition. For every image there is a counter-image: light and dark; stone and flower;

"field trip" and bed. The chapters are contrasted—one ends in violence; the next begins calmly. The characters are deliberately flattened and stylized to convey melodramatic conflict. These various juxtapositions are even more effective because of West's concision. His sentences are so spare that they emphasize the slightest tensions. The result is that *Miss Lonelyhearts* is a wounding experience or, to use West's own phrase, a "religious experience." It makes us see where we are; it refuses to describe new directions.

4

A Cool Million

In *A Cool Million* (1934) West is superficially interested in the social and political dreams of Americans, but even here he indulges in compulsive attacks upon the body and art. Although this novel is not as successful as the preceding ones,[1] it demands some close reading.

The title, we find, is from an "old saying": "John D. Rockefeller would give a cool million to have a stomach like yours." It suggests that money is not enough; a healthy stomach counts. The irony is that in the long run, neither capitalism or health wins. Only death does. The final victory (or "dismantling") continually undercuts the tentative optimism of the old saying.

West begins the novel with a lengthy description of Mrs. Sarah Pitkin's home. Charm is stressed: "An antique collector, had one chanced to pass it by, would have been greatly interested in its arthitecture." But the charm is "outdated," dead, full of clichés. The home— we remember the structures of the two previous novels —functions symbolically; it is a mirror of the quaintness of the American past (dream) and family.

Mrs. Pitkin is a widow with an only son, Lemuel. Again West gives us a one-sided family relationship. His widow is not a ferocious woman like Fay Doyle; she is beyond sex. But she is still domineering enough for Lemuel to seek his fortune with men, rather than women. Underlying the greeting-card tone is an almost

classic case history—one which partially resembles that
of Balso Snell or Miss Lonelyhearts. More of this later!

Mrs. Pitkin and Mr. Slemp confer about the mort-
gage. She is given three months to raise the necessary
monies. If she cannot, the house will be sold to Asa
Goldstein of "Colonial Exteriors and Interiors." West is
vicious toward Goldstein—he links the Jew with the
greedy, commercial world rather than with threatening
religion (as in *The Dream Life of Balso Snell*) [2]—but
he is also nasty toward Mrs. Pitkin. She is an object of
fun; her well-meaning clichés, like those of Miss Lonelyhearts, cannot achieve anything. They are out of place.

Now we meet Lem. He is very close to his mother.
He is described first as "the widow's son"; he has no
personality apart from this identification. When we see
more of him, we discover that he is a "strong spirited
lad" of seventeen. The two adjectives are quite ironic
because he never really displays the strong spirit needed
to conquer the world (or his mother's desires). He
drops the ax he has used to threaten Mr. Slemp. He
rushes to comfort Mother. They sit plunged in gloom.

West uses quick changes of mood (as he does in *The
Dream Life of Balso Snell* and *Miss Lonelyhearts*). He
gives us "charm," "gloom" and finally "desperation."
Lem decides, as the first chapter ends, to see Mr.
Nathan Whipple, the town's most prominent citizen,
who is a former president of the United States. He is the
spiritual father of the town (if not the country itself)
and of the lad. By seeking his advice and power—the
two cannot be separated in the novel—Lem strikes out
on his own. He tries to become a man—if only to save
his mother. The final words of the chapter are "to help
his mother save her home." Not their home!

Mr. Whipple, we discover, lives in a two-story frame
house on the main street which also serves as a place
of business. Here is the location of the "Rat River
National Bank." By again calling attention to the house
as symbol, West emphasizes the difference between Mr.
Whipple and Mrs. Pitkin. The former president mixes

commerce and family life, corrupting the latter in his pursuit of the dollar. We are told "that he had always saved." One of Mr. Whipple's favorite adages is "Don't teach your grandmother to suck eggs." (The novel is filled with sayings—usually these are inverted) West informs us that this means a denial of the pleasures of the body (grandmothers). The analogy is puzzling, even after we finish laughing at it, but perhaps we can interpret it to mean that Mr. Whipple is against the family, close relationships, in his desire to hoard eggs (valuables). He has substituted the country for the family. He is a super patriot, praising the flag every evening: "All hail Old Glory!" Because he is so warm toward it (it is easier to love a symbol than another person), he cannot view it clearly.[3] It becomes a cliché.

Lem, who represents the youth of the nation to Mr. Whipple, asks him now for a loan. He refuses. (although his answer is "surprising" to the boy, we are not surprised; we know him too well to underestimate his deceits.) He suggests that "this is a land of opportunity" and in it can be found wealth. The cliché hides Mr. Whipple's own love of the dollar and his denial of family. But Lem agrees with the great man.

There is broad irony as Mr. Whipple offers his young friend (who has an "honest face") a loan of thirty dollars with Mrs. Pitkin's cow as security. He sends Lem on his way after praising America as the golden land. Then he turns to the picture of Lincoln on the wall and "communes" with it. The picture, like the flag, is worshipped for his own materialistic ends.

In the next chapter Lem, now referred to as our "hero," passes through a forest on the way home. He twirls a "stout stick" he has just cut. The stick is obviously phallic, especially when it is used as a powerful weapon to attack the dog pursuing Betty Prail. Betty is a timid "young lady" who apparently loves Lem; she admires his good nature. The sexual quality of their relationship is not very vital. It is amusing to see the turnabout. Lem is powerful with dog and shy Betty, (the "butcher" boy who owns the dog) or Mr. Whipple, but when he has to deal with a bully like Tom Baxter he becomes a weakling. Here is the secret. Lem is too aware of the rules (clichés) to realize that he must go beyond them. He must make his own rules in this land of opportunity. He is defeated by Baxter (who squeezes him "insensible") because he is so obedient and sportsmanlike. His dismantling has already begun.[4]

In the next chapter the narrator gives us some more background material about Miss Prail. (West does not describe the motives of this narrator; he merely allows him to talk in clichés. Are we to assume that "I" is the voice of America?) She is an orphan. When she was twelve, her farm was destroyed by fire. The firemen (including Bill Baxter, the father of Tom) arrived there completely drunk. They looted the place. Bill raped her. The rape is amusing in a grim way; it also underlines the greed of the firemen. No object is sacred except the dollar! Betty was sent to the Slemp family after a stay in the orphan asylum.

We would expect Lawyer Slemp to be as duplicitous as Mr. Whipple. We are not very disturbed to learn that he beat Betty "regularly and enthusiastically." (Violence and sex are always married in West's sadomasochistic novels.) But we laugh after discovering that Betty doesn't mind the beating, especially when she receives a quarter each time. It seems as if victims—like their masters—will do anything for money.

It is characteristic of this novel to wander. The narrator drifts in and out; Lem moves from place to place; small incidents are belabored. Once we accept such wandering, we don't mind the disappearance of Betty for a while as, in the next chapter, we again meet Lem. He regains consciousness—has he ever been conscious? —and walks home. He lies to his "fond" mother about the reasons for his lateness. Has he joined the other powerful confidence men he has met? No! He just does not want to worry her. She is certain that he will succeed in his new life.

"Bright and early" next morning—the adjectives typically reflect the sunny disposition of the hero—Lem goes to the local depot to wait for his train to New York City. (He stops on the way to give Mr. Whipple a note for the thirty dollars minus interest.) His adventures begin. When he meets a "stylishly dressed" young man, we expect trouble. The adjectives suggest a confidence man. Mr. Wellington Mape—to rhyme with rape?—is so suave and polite that Lem actually believes that he is kin to the Mayor of New York; he does not notice the man stealing the thirty dollars in his wallet. The entire incident is not very subtle, to say the least, but it does imply that Lem is so involved with money-earning schemes (but for a noble cause!) that he cannot see anything clearly. It also contains West's first reference to the title: Mr. Mape contends that he need not work because his father has left him "a cool million."

After he discovers the theft, Lem also finds that through an error, the "crook" dropped a diamond ring into his pocket. He is saved! But not for long! Another shady character, claiming to be a pawnbroker, buys the ring for much less than it is worth. The turns of fortune are slightly inventive, but they are so mechanical and easy. When the police enter the scene to arrest Lem, the action becomes more interesting. They are drawn broadly as villians—like the false Mr. Whipple or Lawyer Slemp, they are hated "fathers." West violently describes their violence: they catch Lem roughly; they strike "extremely hard blows"; they kick him in the stomach with heavy boots. They are frightening (unlike Mr. Mape) because they are beyond the law. They join the firemen who defiled Betty. I believe that West is effective in these scenes because he identifies with Lem. He cannot live in a fatherless society.

West's hatred for the establishment—to use the current word—extends, of course, to the warden of the state prison to which Lem is sent. Although he is stern, he is also kind. He benevolently suggests that his "son" have cold showers [5] — "cold water is an excellent cure for morbidity" — and teeth extraction. Thus the physical "dismantling" begins (after the mental turmoil of the preceding chapters). This dismantling is a significant aspect of the novel; it even supplies the subtitle, *The Dismantling of Lemuel Pitkin*. West was so concerned with the body, as I have stressed, that it represents freedom and determinism. It is a holy totem, carrying with (or in) it the various answers to human abstractions. Freedom; responsibility; art — such things are viewed mainly in relation to the body. By focusing on physical dismantling, West gives a sense of urgency to his comedy. He paints the comedy black, redeeming it from easy social satire of Wall Street or flag-worship. He evokes primitive responses in us; he makes us terrified children once more — we identify (in part) with his "hero."

But West pauses. He does not pursue the physical dismantling for the time being — can't he face it? — and turns instead to Betty Prail. She is a double (or, better yet, "sister") of Lem. She is also in the dark — she is now lying on the bottom of a wagon taking her to a whorehouse in New York City.

Perhaps the most interesting aspect of this chapter (aside from the clumsy, stupid attacks by West upon Italians and Chinese) is the lengthy description of Betty's new home. Wu Fong's establishment is dream-like (as it caters to men's dreams). The rooms are furnished in different styles: Directoire, Spanish, and colonial American. The styles are Hollywood clichés (preparing us for the more substantial ones of West's Hollywood novel), but they mirror in an inverted way, the folksy styles of Mr. Whipple and Mrs. Pitkin. The question is: Why should the American dream be centered only in Mrs. Pitkin's house? West uses Wu Fong's establishment (and the fact that Betty is "colonial") to attack all houses — houses of ill fame and good name!

There is a related implication. West spends so much

space on interior decoration that it becomes more important than Betty or her "comic" predicament. Physical objects dominate personality. They indeed, determine it. West subtly implies that they, like the body of Lem, are the real protagonists of the novel.

The narrator switches to Lem. He first emphasizes the body—the bad case of pneumonia; the false teeth —before he reintroduces Mr. Whipple, who has landed in prison because of "the un-American conspiracy" of Wall Street and the Communists. (An odd couple.) But both are reborn again as they reaffirm their faith in America. They will invent something to make a cool million. Note the intermingling of personal optimism— we can do anything!—and the powerful invention; it is man and machine again.

Lem leaves prison, finds a new home in a Bowery hotel, and visits Asa Goldstein's Colonial Exteriors and Interiors. Here he views his old home. The house is now seedy—it can never be the same for him!—and its condition is curiously valuable. Lem enhances the value by informing the clerks about the proper (authentic!) setting for pieces of furniture to be placed in it. Unwittingly he becomes a salesman. His adventures continue as in saving Mr. Levi Underdown and daughter from a runaway horse, he injures his eye. This cloudy vision is symbolically right. It does not enable him to see the return of Mr. Wellington Mape as Sylvanus Snodgrasse, the poet.

This confidence man is not particularly interesting, as I have already said, but he does give an intriguing sermon about heroism and poetry. It is a set piece. It incoherently pleads for social symbols; it demands that we honor the heroic acts of the common man. But it is, finally, a ruse to divert the hearers from pickpockets at work. Does the speech contain some of the problems plaguing West? Does West imply that heroism is impossible in a country dominated by machines and pickpockets? Is this the reason for his surrender to the clichés he vehemently assaults? Can he view heroism merely as a final ruse or diversion? These questions are raised by Snodgrasse's sermon (and the novel itself), but like the narrative technique, they wander aimlessly.

The funny coincidences continue. Several weeks after the incident, Lem leaves the hospital "minus his right eye." (It had been severely damaged.) He stands on a corner, not knowing which way to turn. He sees Mr. Whipple, who is dressed in a "coonskin hat." Mr. Whipple is a more sinister figure now. He is no longer the odd, private ex-president we met at the beginning of the novel. He is putting his social ideas into action by founding a "new party with the old American principles." The National Revolutionary Party is his dream and, like the dreams offered for sale by Wu Fong and Asa Goldstein, it caters to the desire for romantic clichés. It is popular art.[6] The uniform is a deerskin shirt, a pair of moccasins, and the coonskin hat; the weapon is a squirrel rifle. The party carries religious burden as it preaches salvation (from Wall Street and communism) and immortality (of the American way).[7] Mr. Whipple is fittingly, called a "priest"; he makes Lem his disciple.

The two men face the crowd near the Salvation Army canteen. They chant "famous slogans." Mr. Whipple, like Shrike or the would-be artists in *The Dream Life of Balso Snell,* launches into a sermon. Instead of Christ or Art he praises America: "We alone are American; and when we die, America dies." But the principles are similar. "America" is a cliché used to convert the masses—to renew their faith. Chief Jake Raven, one of the vagrants, steps forward to proclaim his new-found belief. He is an Indian. His dark skin bothers Mr. Whipple, but he is finally accepted as an authentic believer. So the crusade begins.

In the crowd is a "remarkable," fat person. He wears spats, a "tight-fitting Chesterfield overcoat" with a black velvet collar. He is the spy. He calls two secret phone exchanges—one for Wall Street; the other for Communists—and soon after both groups send officers to

break up the meeting. It is a curious development because we are forced to assume that Mr. Whipple is
somewhat justified in his paranoia—we are suddenly
shaken by new evidence. West is at fault here; he makes
him a rational character, harming his satire.

Our disappointments continue. In the next chapter
West again introduces the confidence-man routine. Lem
goes to work for Elmer Hainey, Esquire, who forces him
to wear a glass eye and expensive clothes, and to visit
jewelry stores where he will claim that he has lost his
eye. Our interest is maintained less by the scheme (or
Mr. Hainey) than by the further "dismantling" of Lem.
He is seen here as a "bundle of old rags." His clothes will
not be able to hide his more-ragged condition.

His new job reminds him of "amateur theatricals."
The phase underlines the performances in the novel.
Everyone acts a role (or is *directed* to act one).[8] Mr.
Whipple is Spiritual Father; Lem is Helpless Victim; the
confidence men assume various identities. Thus theater,
commerce, and politics merge in an outrageous (but not
outrageous enough!) show.

In Chinatown (where everyone seems to put on a
performance of sorts) Lem ventures near Wu Fong's
establishment. The union with Betty will soon take
place. Before West really develops the plot he again
turns to the interior decoration. He lovingly elaborates
it. We see Pennsylvania Dutch, Old South, Log Cabin
Pioneer, etc. The rooms (designed, of course, by Asa
Goldstein) match the various whores (or vice versa).
We have already got the joke; we are bored this second
time even though he meticulously describes such details as the girls' names and costumes.

Lem reads the note Betty has just thrown out of Wu
Fong's house. He is set to rescue her, but he is captured
by an enormous Chinaman. The racist clichés abound
in the description of the latter: he uses skillful oriental
tricks; he whistles through his nose in "coolie fashion";
he is obedient. Wu Fong is "crafty." The Indian prince
who pays for Lem (now a male prostitute!) does not

escape incest clichés: he leers, he lusts, and he lisps. The racism is meant to add to the humor, but it destroys it. It is not as darkly comic as the continuing destruction of Lem.

West cannot control himself. In the next chapter he proceeds to attack Irish police (they are stupid and violent), Jewish attorneys (they are sly and corrupt), New England types (they see guilt in everyone). The nasty silliness harms the novel but it does even more—it affirms that West is so angry at the American dream-cheat that he himself believes in some sort of conspiracy. He succumbs, as it were, to a latent fascism without even realizing it.[9] He is on the way to joining Mr. Whipple's party.

After Lem is released from prison—he goes to prison so often that it almost replaces the family home—he is approached by a streetwalker smelling of cheap perfume. It is Betty. When they recognize each other, they are shocked at the changes they have suffered. But in this anticliché novel which lapses into cliché, they somehow retain their optimism. They can survive failure! They love each other!

The plot thickens with the return of indestructible Mr. Whipple and Jake Raven. They are going West to dig gold and finance the further activities of the National Revolutionary Party. Betty and Lem travel with them. In Chicago (between trains) Lem falls into the hands of a bearded stranger (we have met him before), a spy for the Third International. They fight. The outcome is not surprising. Lem is injured. He feels "as though he were being whirled rapidly through a dark tunnel full of clanging bells." He forces the ambulance which has been sent for him to rush him back to the train station just in time for his scheduled departure with the others. He is still optimistic! He is still stupid!

They arrive in California and set up residence in a log cabin. They now become mirrors of the original pioneers. Perhaps their violence—the novel's tempo accelerates from here to the end—reflects the spirit of their landscape. (The country is more violent than the city.) Their first visitor is a caricature of Daniel Boone and other folk heroes. He carries a knife and two pearl-handled revolvers; he drinks; he boasts that he "can tackle a lion without flinchin.'" His bloodthirsty declarations are comic at first, but the more we see of him, the more terrified we are of his random rage. He is not to be laughed at (in the same way we laugh at Mr. Wellington Mape or even Mr. Whipple). His anarchy resembles the forces of law and order West has previously described. The point is clear: the Missouri man (the outlaw) and the authorities resemble each other — the helpless victim, Lem or Betty, is caught between them. The sense of community begins to fade as the various pioneers turn upon one another.

The Missouri man calls Jake Raven names. Mr. Whipple regards him with anxiety. Lem is uneasy. One of the high points of the novel occurs when the Missouri man tells an anecdote about how his best friend disagreed with him. Their dispute led to murder: "I'm the rip-tail roarer from Pike County, Missouri, and no man can insult me and live. 'Jack,' says I, 'we've been friends, but you've insulted me, and you must pay with your life.' Then I up with my iron and shot him through the head." We expect more murder when we note the tensions among our pioneers.

We get it. In the next chapter Lem discovers Jake Raven shot through the chest and the Missouri man trying to rape Betty. He raises an ax to kill him. Our hero is again unsuccessful. (He can't do anything right!) He steps into an enormous bear trap; its "saw toothed jaws closed with great force" on his legs. The trap is, perhaps, a symbol of the entire world which has been conspiring to catch him since he left home. He falls "in a heap." The Missouri man cooly continues his actions, accomplishing his purpose and leaves.[10]

Although West ridicules the primitivistic slogans of the Indians — to whom Jake goes for help — we cannot completely assent to his name-calling. The Indian chief may be silly when he says that the white man has "loused the continent up good," but he echoes one of the novel's themes in attacking that violence which is called progress. He speaks of the paleface rotting "this land in the name of progress"; filling the rivers with refuse; and flooding the country with "toilet paper, painted boxes to keep pins in, key rings, watch fobs, leatherette satchels." [11] The chief's sermon—another one to add to our list!—is surprisingly contemporary. Not only is he for ecology—he is also for fighting violence with violence! He urges his people to "smash" the clock: "The time is ripe. Riot and profaneness, poverty and violence are everywhere." They ride forward.

It is only when we see the results of the chief's sermon that we agree with West. The Indians tear the scalp of, you guessed it, Lem Pitkin, "looting his bloody head of its store teeth and glass eye." Their violence knows no bounds; it mixes friend and foe so that "the fire this time" engulfs the innocent.

West is even more ironic toward Lem's spiritual father. He can excuse the Indians somewhat because he considers them "savages," but he cannot let Mr. Whipple's narcissistic importance go unnoticed. Mr. Whipple gives Lem oranges, wild flowers (as the youth's leg is removed at the knee); he wants to use him for his own gain: "Why not get a tent and exhibit his young friend as the last man to have been scalped by the Indians? . . ."

Lem becomes more of an object than he was previously. He has been a glass eye, a set of teeth—West has concentrated upon his physical parts, not his mental condition—but now he loses whatever substance (or personality) he had. He becomes a sideshow freak.

The show draws crowds—always eager to gape at dreams or nightmares—but they are not sufficient to keep it running. Mr. Whipple and Lem seek other employment. They start working for Snodgrasse, who conveniently appears in order to tie the plot threads together. They do not know that he is really an agent for the conspiracy of Wall Street and communism.

Enough of the plot here! West is more interested in the "Chamber of American Horrors, Animate and Inanimate Hideosities" than in the reasons for Mr. Whipple, Snodgrasse, or Lem joining it. In his description of the "inanimate horrors" he reaches the high art of his previous novels. He realizes that by emphasizing the usual marriage of objects and people (or objects), he can attack the terrifying clichés which surround us. Thus he gives us "a Venus de Milo with a clock in her abdomen, a copy of Power's *Greek Slave* with elastic bandages on all her joints, a Hercules weaving a small compact truss." There are several reasons for his choice: 1] He suggests that we Americans confuse art and commerce, debasing the former. We must make Venus de Milo do something for profit; she cannot merely be. (She is compared symbolically with Lem; both are "deformed" by profiteering businessmen.)   2] He suggests that we are preoccupied (and he should know!) by the body. We tend to "idolize" sickness, spending so much time and money upon it that we distrust health or beauty. We enslave ourselves (thus the *Greek Slave*).   3] We are unable to perceive anything clearly; we merge reality and unreality.   4] We love objects more than people. The inanimate horrors are a microcosm of the horrors attacked in the entire novel.

West keeps going. He shows us a "gigantic hemorrhoid that was lit from within by electric lights." (Think of *The Dream Life of Balso Snell*.) One wall displays "collections of objects whose distinction lay in the great skill with which their materials had been disguised." Paper looks like wood; wood like rubber, etc. These objects reinforce the duplicity theme. If objects can resemble other objects, they can also resemble people—indeed, dominate them. Is Lem Pitkin more than a glass eye or false teeth? Does America allow people to be more than objects?

The "animate" part of the show consists of a "pageant." Short sketches involving the manipulation or torture of Quakers, Negroes, and Indians are performed. West tells us ironically that Snodgrasse fails to connect this part with the inanimate part; the relationship is clear enough as I have suggested. We are not informed which comes first but in all probability the enslavement of people (that is, as objects) is the cause.

West tries to give us a "playlet" as a culmination of the show. He presents a "sleek salesman" trying to sell "Grandmother" worthless bonds; "Grandmother" and three small sons dying of starvation in the street; and two millionaires gloating over their counterfeit bonds. The "playlet" is not as convincing as the imaged objects; we would expect this to be the case because the novel itself is effective only in metaphor and image, not in characterization.

In Detroit, Lem and Mr. Whipple discuss the implications of the show (in which they still perform). Mr. Whipple insists that there is a distinction between "good" and "bad" capitalists—a Henry Ford is creative; the "international banker"—does he mean Jew? —is not. He hopes that the show continues even in this city which is un-American (containing, as it does, "Jews, Catholics and members of unions"). He bides his time.

When they reach Beulah, a real American town, Mr. Whipple rises to the occasion. He gets all the inhabitants who do not belong to minority groups to assemble for his speech. (Of course, they carry a rope or a gun!) He begins peacefully, claiming to love the South because "her women are beautiful and chaste, her men brave and gallant. . . ." Then he declares his love of America. Now the violence begins! Mr. Whipple says that the time has come for action—an enemy "threatens our freedom." He urges his heroic followers to get up and slay foes. Although these clichés are not particularly new, they are still pertinent, especially if we see Mr. Whipple with us now. I wish, however, that West's rhetoric were more chilling and expressive. Only when he mentions "the heroes considered their lack of knowledge an advantage rather than a hindrance, for it gave them a great deal of leeway in their choice of a victim, . . ." does he capture the mindless violence of the situation.

Words turn into deeds. The citizens "loot the principal stores"; free their jail-bound relatives; cut off the heads of Negroes; rape a Catholic housekeeper; and nail a Jewish "drummer" to his hotel room door. This "physical dismantling" echoes in a more general way the lonely plight of Lem. Private nightmares have become social phenomena!

When the meeting breaks up, Lem is separated from Mr. Whipple and his followers. (He is suspected of being an enemy.) He returns to New York City and, in one of the fine details which almost redeem the novel, he finds that his "ragged, emaciated appearance," helps him to "submerge himself in the great army of unemployed." He is not alone! He joins his dismantled brothers!

Lem gets a job—it is difficult to place him because of his many missing parts!—with a vaudeville team named Riley and Robbins. He is "the *object* [my italics] of merriment." West tells us that from "a not very civilized" viewpoint, he qualifies for such a position. This is the idea—the times, the country, and life itself are "not very civilized." They demand such descriptions as the following: "Instead of merely having no hair like a man prematurely bald, the gray bone of his skull showed plainly where he had been scalped by Chief Satinpenny. Then, too, his wooden leg had been carved with initials, twined hearts and other innocent insignia had not seen him previously). The description is, per by mischievous boys." We see Lem in full view (as we had not seen him previously). The description is, perhaps, even more shocking because his new parts have been defaced. No wonder that the comics exclaim: "You're a wow!"

Lem performs that very night. He stands between the comics; he wears a baggy Prince Albert; he looks extremely sober and dignified. He is then assaulted by

Riley and Robbins, who try to "knock off his toupee or to knock out his teeth and eye." When they succeed, Lem replaces "the things that had been knocked off or out." The performance builds toward "The Works." For the final curtain he is "completely demolished."

The "not very civilized" audience laughs (as we do?). They regard Lem as the stooge or the dummy. His feelings are forgotten. He is an "inanimate" comedy. We consider him in a more complex way, however, because we have known him. We recognize the roots of his condition. Thus we stand apart from the audience, noting its violent, inhuman behavior. We hate it as it hates (or laughs at) Lem.

The ultimate dismantling occurs just as Mr. Whipple gains in power. His forces riot; he demands dictatorship. West juxtaposes the fall and rise, connecting these events in our minds. He suggests that America is a see-saw which will not rest.

The final chapter is probably the most sustained piece of writing in the novel (except for the passages on interior decoration). A stranger comes to see Lem and addresses him as "Commander Pitkin." Will he consent to speak to the crowds in the theater on behalf of the National Revolutionary Party? Although Lem claims that he is not a "real actor" but only a "stooge," he agrees because his heart belongs to Mr. Whipple.

Lem walks onto the stage alone. He wears the "dress uniform of the 'Leather Shirts,' " but the audience still roars with laughter. Our poor hero tries to speak: he claims that he is a clown. He does not finish. He is drilled through the heart—the final wounding—by a bullet from his old foe, the "fat fellow in the Chester-field overcoat."

But the novel does not end here. There is no silence at this point. West ironically demonstrates the resurrection of Lem as national hero. He is made a martyr by Mr. Whipple. (Even in death he is used to play a role.) He is sung about in "The Lemuel Pitkin Song": "A million hearts for Pitkin, oh!" His mother gains glory; so does Betty Prail (who reappears now as his loyal sweetheart).

Mr. Whipple has the last word. He delivers a eulogy (as Shrike did for Miss Lonelyhearts). He calls him "great." He finds that he personified "the right of every American boy to go into the world and there receive fair play." He did not die in vain! We know better.

The last words of the novel are "All hail, the American boy!" They make us remember that Lem is an unsuccessful allegorical figure used by West to stand for youth and America. He cannot bear such a burden of meaning (as he could not carry Mr. Whipple, Snodgrasse, and the others), but in his fall, he makes us think of other, more heroic figures suddenly cut down.

It is fortunate that West is able to end *A Cool Million* in such a powerful way. The ending—actually the last thirty pages or so—compels us to cloud over the silliness of most of the novel—the racist slurs; the juvenile dialogue; the unwitting descent into clichés (as they are attacked)—and, indeed, to persuade us that it is somehow "intentional." Such misreading and wishful thinking does a disservice to West. We should see the novel clearly as a misguided, faulty effort—an attempt to write a light-hearted piece of propaganda. Propaganda, black comedy, and allegory do not usually mix.

A Cool Million will be read for its nightmarish insights into mass violence and physical decay. It is full of "dismantling"; when it strays from this obsession, it becomes uneven and false, turning into self-righteous cliché.

5

The Day of the Locust

In *The Day of the Locust* (1939) West is on more solid ground. He is at his best here (and, of course, in *Miss Lonelyhearts*) because he refrains from silly propaganda and limits his attention to one closely knit group. He is "claustrophobic," tight, and narrow—although less so than in *Miss Lonelyhearts*. I will again explicate the novel in chronological sequence, hoping that such exploration takes us to the heart of the matter.

The novel begins with noise—a "great din" is heard outside the window. There is the "jangle of iron," the "groan of leather." It seems as if the whole world is falling apart. The next paragraph helps us to see the source of noise. (Although West begins with hearing, he swiftly turns to seeing: The novel is determinedly visual.) We stare at an army which moves "like a mob." But we are shocked to notice the quaint costumes—the shakos, the dolmans—and the odd weapons. Things are "jumbled together in bobbing disorder." This disorder is strengthened when we see at the end of the paragraph, the "Scotch with bare knees under plaid skirts." We are suddenly disoriented. What is happening? Quickly we discover that the army is "unreal." It is directed by a "little fat man" who calls it "bastards." It moves to "Stage Nine." It appears to be defeated.

The contrast between the real and the unreal is, of course, familiar. We have noted it in the earlier novels, but we see it more developed, if this is possible, in

Hollywood, the "dream factory." The violence (and noise) is expected. So is the emphasis upon the grotesque and comic—the fat man in "pursuit of the army" and defeating it.

After the army retreats, we remember that we have seen it through someone's eyes. Tod Hackett is the observer. His name is deceptively simple. Once we start "free associating," we find powerful symbolic resonances. Tod—death in German? Hackett—hack it? The all-American name contains potentialities for violence and destruction. Tod hears the noise outside; he is separated from it (for the present) by a shield—a window. As the novel progresses, he will become part of it. The window resembles the eye (and the camera). It can be hurt or broken from the outside. Tod hears the noise at "quitting time"; it intrudes at a time of peace, relaxation, or passivity—that is, when least expected. The detail is symbolic. It suggests that our observer (our eye?) cannot quit.

Tod leaves the office after putting away his pencils and drawing board. He is an artist (like Balso Snell and Miss Lonelyhearts), but he is also a performer.[1] He cannot remain outside, totally removed from the action. He will join the "army" later.

We now get his past in a flashback. He was hired by telegram; some of his drawings had led a talent scout to recruit him. He has been in Hollywood for less than three months. It is no wonder that he is confused about his place in the system. He knows as little as we do; he is our spiritual brother. As he learns, we learn.

Tod's appearance echoes that of the army. It does not seem to belong to an artist. His eyes; his "sloppy grin"; his large body—such details make him "seem completely without talent."[2] Tod is said to be a "very complicated young man"—most unlike Lemuel Pitkin! —with a "whole set of personalities." This description is somewhat odd. What exactly does a "whole set of personalities" mean? Is it desirable to have it? Is one personality truer than the others? Such questions are intriguing in a novel of unreality. There is one other detail about Tod. He is painting "The Burning of Los Angeles." It will prove that despite his physical appearance, he has great talent.

Tod walks along and again stares at others. Now it is another "army." It also consists of dreamlike figures, wearing clothes that do not fit the occasion. The girl in slacks has just left "a switchboard, not a tennis court." The man with a sports hat is returning from an insurance office. These "masquerades"—the word is carefully chosen by West—are joined by more somber figures who have no place to go. These loiter; they stare at the workers returning home.

Tod is determined to learn more about the somber figures so that he can paint them (and give them life?). He cannot paint any longer like Winslow Homer; he turns to Goya and Daumier for inspiration. Hollywood itself will be his canvas (and subject). Tod studies the landscape. Night falls. Things become eerie. The declining light resembles a "Neon tube"—remember the hemorrhoid in *A Cool Million!*—and it almost makes the ugly hills look beautiful (as art can transform the grotesque into the beautiful; see *Miss Lonelyhearts*). But the dusk does little for the jumble of architectural styles—ranch houses, chalets, Tudor cottages and the rest. The houses are made of plaster and paper; they are stage sets, as it were, and they can repeat no law. They are completely unreal.

Tod does not laugh. Like Miss Lonelyhearts he realizes that the houses are dream palaces for beauty and romance—they cannot be merely camp. They inspire sighs because they are "truly monstrous." The thought is shocking. We usually think of the monstrous as alien; Tod and West find its sources in a need for romance; the need redeems the monstrous, making it all too human and sympathetic.[3]

In the next chapter Tod enters his apartment house. The facade resembles the style of the other houses he has just studied—it is "Moorish" pink and dark yellow in color. It is called the "San Bernandino Arms," but it still remains a "non-descript affair." (We have come a long way from Lem's humble dwelling!) [4]

He pauses to catch a glimpse of Faye Greener—whom we shall soon meet—but he is not in luck. He gets to his room, takes off his jacket, and lies on his bed. (We wonder whether he will be another reclining Balso Snell or Miss Lonelyhearts). He looks through the window—the motif recurs—and sees "a square of enameled sky." Even nature seems made-up, slick, and hard.

Tod thinks of his painting—Art, rather than Nature, concerns him—and one of his subjects, "Honest Abe Kusich." Abe is said to be one of the "Dancers" (along with Faye Greener), performing for "the group of uneasy people" who form the audience. There is hostility between audience and performer (as there is in all of the novels)—the audience stares so much that Abe and the others "spin crazily." Their contortions make them resemble "hooked trout." Perhaps the dancers resemble the army manipulated by the fat man?

Tod remembers his first view of Abe. He had lived in a hotel called the Chateau Mirabella—the name wonderfully captures the romance of Hollywood—which was mainly inhabited by hustlers of all sorts. One night he was going to his room, when he saw a "pile of soiled laundry" opposite his door. The pile moved—it was a tiny man. He was dressed in a "woman's flannel bathrobe"—West characteristically chooses confused sexual identity—and he groaned.

Abe's first words were "The hell you say." He showed great anger. His anger, we can say, was inversely proportional to his size. He threatened Tod and the woman whose bathrobe he wore. (His hostility toward the "bitch" is our introduction to sex in the novel.[5] It suggests that West will again describe sex as warfare.) Then he suddenly became friendly, asking Tod if he could dress in his place. The displacement of the first chapter is echoed here by Abe's lack of a room and Tod's unhappiness over his own.

Abe dressed. The Tyrolean hat he put on had a "magic green color"; it did not go well with the blue, double-breasted suit and the black shirt. His costume— the word is carefully chosen—was somehow so garish that it was "perfect"—a perfect example of the "truly monstrous" in its need to assert itself. Abe continued to "act," using slang. He personified toughness (if one forgot his size!).

Abe offered advice. Why not bet five on a horse at the track? He knew the horse would win. His confidence waned as he remembered the bitch who threw him out. The range from omniscience to rage is crazy. Abe moved so quickly that he did not seem in control of himself (let alone horses, women, or Tod). He suddenly left the room and rushed down the hall.

Abe appeared again a few days later. He considered himself "an expert" on housing and told Tod to move to the "San Bernandino Arms." When the advice was not taken at first, he became violent. (His manhood was at stake!) But he prevailed, and Tod, like the other passive heroes of West, allowed "himself to be bullied." Honest Abe won. (Does West mean him to be a Jew? Does he mean to imply nastily that Jews always give advice and have much self-importance for their size?)

The third chapter returns us to the present. Tod gets up and dresses in front of the mirror. The mirror is a kind of window in which he stands outside himself. His separation is stressed for the present. But even here his eyes stray to the photograph of Faye Greener. (It is appropriate that we first see her as "still-life." Even when she appears in person, she is on film, as it were— an object to behold!) The photograph shows her as an "extra" (as all the characters are); she is dressed in a "harem costume," holding incongruously a beer bottle and a stein.

Her appearance is significant. She has "swordlike" legs—West suggests her man-killing abilities with the phallic image—platinum hair, moon face, but these various features go together in the right kind of way.

She is vital, beautiful, cruel. She lies on the divan looking drugged and somehow ready. For what? Not pleasure!

Tod turns away from the photograph, but after lighting a cigarette nervously, he returns to it. He wants to enter it (and Faye), to break through the window. Her expression is an invitation to murder (or suicide): "If you threw yourself on her, it would be like throwing yourself from the parapet of a skyscraper." She incarnates the death-wish. It is significant that she is Faith (her first name); both are murderous and deceptive in Hollywood (which, in itself, is a pun on holy wood). Tod laughs at his language and like Beagle Darwin, laughs at his laugh. His laughter is also linked to destruction—befitting a novel which begins with an "army"—but he realizes it isn't a "real laugh and nothing [is] destroyed by it."

Tod goes to a party at Claude Estee's. The expedition resembles the field trips of Miss Lonelyhearts in that it offers more frustration than staying at home. Claude Estee is a successful screen writer because he, unlike Tod, belongs to Hollywood. He performs the correct role—wears the right mask—for his audience. He impersonates a Civil War colonel to go along with the Southern architecture of his mansion: he screams for a mint julep (his Chinese servant comes running with a Scotch); he elaborates an accent. But there is more to Claude—as we shall see.

Tod meets the other guests. Mrs. Schwartzen has an eighteen-year-old face and a thirty-five-year-old neck (talk about mixture!); she flutters her eyelids; she "adores smut." Some producers talk shop about Easterners who can not get along in Hollywood (like Tod?). The unreality of the guests finds its objective correlative in the physical description. Tod sees the "blue serge sky" (nature as fabric) and the moon that resembles "a bone button" (nature as material), but he is especially startled to see a "life-size, realistic reproduction" of a dead horse in the swimming pool. The horse's mouth is set in "an agonized grin." Consider the mixture of life and death, pain and laughter, reality and unreality; the horse carries many of the symbolic marriages in the entire novel. It is, furthermore, very expensive!

After Tod leaves Mrs. Schwartzen (who wants to "cherish her illusions") and the producers (who continue to talk about their "racket"), he sits down in the library with Claude. They talk about Alice Jenning's brothel. Claude likes it because it's a "triumph of industrial design." It is "skillful packaging." (It is close to his own success as a screen writer.) Tod claims that like all brothels, it will be depressing—it'a only a place for deposit. He cites "mail boxes, tombs," etc. He seems to have West's characteristic obsession with places of entrapment (including the body?). Claude takes up the metaphor, playing with it until he sounds like a *Balso Snell* performer or Shrike. He mixes body and machine—"bowels of the device"; love as vending machine. There is again the emphasis upon reality and unreality.

Tod steers the conversation to his own plight regarding Faye Greener (although he does not mention her name). He has been chasing a girl—it's like "carrying something a little too large to conceal in your pocket, like a briefcase or a small valise." His simile is odd—the reason for it is unclear. Claude just moves ahead with it. The valise (as the desire to have the girl?) changes shape. It becomes foreign. These various games with serious passion debase it, making it mechanical or superficial. This is West's intention. Claude (more than Tod who plays straight man) sees other people, serious passion, and the world itself as raw material for film. He must cheapen or flatten them for the average guy, the "barber in Purdue," knowing all the while that he is exploiting him. He sighs heavily as he recognizes that he can no longer separate himself from that barber, the serious from the trivial. In a sense he is the rubber horse!

Mrs. Jenning is described at some length in the next

chapter. She had once been an actress in silent films, but when sound was introduced, she was put out of work. She switched easily from Hollywood romance to operating the brothel. Now she is particular: she chooses her girls (and their men) carefully; she designs her house tastefully; and she is "cultured," always discussing Gertrude Stein.[6]

Tod and the others proceed to watch a blue movie, *Le Predicament de Marie*. They "imitate a rowdy audience in the days of the nickelodeon." (The imitations are endless; they imitate the audience; the blue movie imitates their dreams; the house itself imitates the movie.) Finally they see the movie—Marie goes through various maneuvers; she is involved with all the members of the family she serves. She is constantly disturbed and frustrated. Then the machine sticks. There are several reasons for West's inclusion of the movie. He suggests by it that there is a close connection between the clichés of pornography and business. The observers regard Marie and her friends as sexual objects, not as people. (We remember Lemuel Pitkin as object.) They are separated from the performance. But as we have noted with Tod, they want (unconsciously?) to break through the window, the film. They are frustrated— more so than Marie?—because they make believe that they are beyond pornography. The movie-within-a-movie-novel is a mirror device which is characteristic of West's fiction. We need think only of the doubles in *The Dream Life of Balso Snell* and *Miss Lonelyhearts*, the story-within-stories of both.

Tod separates himself from the "mock riot" when the machine sticks. He continually tries to be apart for the sake of objectivity. He walks into a room which contains a large number of "miniature dogs" made of glass, silver, and aluminum. These, like Claude's rubber horse, reinforce the ambiguous nature of things—nature as metal again. But Tod, symbolically, cannot remain alone. He goes back to "see the rest of the film." We do not see it. (Maybe West wants to frustrate us.) [7]

A few days later Tod visits Harry Greener, the father of Faye, in the hope of gaining her gratitude and, eventually, her body. The old man is a "clown." His clownship is a "clue"—a painter's clue—and it is linked to Faye's dreams.

West elaborates on Harry's past career. We learn that he first began working on the stage forty years ago. He wore a special costume, dressing like a "cheap, unconvincing, imitation banker." He did not fool anyone with his outfit. (Note the concern again with costume and imitation.) From his clippings—more of this later—we read that Harry was a Lemuel Pitkin. He was kicked in the belly; he limped; and he fell flat on his face. The audience—as in *A Cool Million* and *The Dream Life of Balso Snell*—loved the pain and cruelty. Why does West use clippings? They resemble a window (a film) in that they separate the person; they make him news —"objective," cold, almost dead. The transition from the journalistic portrait to the real (?) person is shocking (even more so than the difference between Miss Lonely-hearts as newspaper columnist and person?).

Harry came to Hollywood, hoping to earn a living in films. But he was unsuccessful. He "stank from hunger" —to use his words. He took to selling silver polish. The detail is significant. The polish disguises dirt, making things pretty once more. So do Hollywood movies.

Tod remembers meeting Homer Simpson on one of his expeditions to Harry. He was keeping the old man company when a man who "seemed an exact·model for the kind of person who comes to California to die," paid a call with wine for Harry and flowers for Faye. The suitor was Homer. (His name ironically marries classical wisdom and simpleton behavior.) He left without saying anything. His silence continued until Tod offered sympathy.

The fact that West introduces both Harry and Homer in the same chapter may be intentional. Perhaps he wants us to associate the two. They are failures, having left or never entered Hollywood society (unlike Mrs.

Jenning of the previous chapter). They are dead. Their condition ironically juxtaposes that of Faye (the center of their attention) as "Nature Goddess." The matter is more complicated because Tod is drawn as much, if not more, to them than to Faye. They are "clues"—to use West's word—to his paintings and, what he does not yet realize, to his life. They are the extremes of his desire for separateness. They symbolically gain strength as he fades in the chapter.

Homer is the center of the following chapters. We are startled to discover that he replaces Tod. Although West regards him as a type (the person who comes to California to die), he does not convince us that he is worth our complete attention—he is less interesting and unusual than the artist. The novel wanders at this point (although not as much as A *Cool Million*).

Many critics have demonstrated that Homer is a grotesque, strongly indebted to Sherwood Anderson, but they have not completely explored his relationship to the imagery of the novel.[8] His grotesque qualities are reinforced—if not created—by the objects surrounding him. He resembles, for example, the insects close to his house—especially the lizard—because he is a crawling thing. (I have noted West's fondness for animal imagery —the hooked trout, the horse. This fondness tends to debase humanity, closing the gap between it and lower forms of life.)[9] He also resembles the house: he is "queer," made of materials that do not go together successfully—"not really straw but heavy fireproof paper colored and ribbed to look like straw." The house is romantic, dreamlike, full of clichés—it contains wall fixtures in the "shape of galleons," red velvet draperies, colonial beds upstairs. Is it any wonder that Homer is grotesque? He reflects—and becomes—his surroundings.

Homer sits in his living room and then in his bedroom. (We are in the midst of an extended flashback in the next chapter.) His passivity reminds us of Miss Lonelyhearts' bedridden position—if not of Lemuel's dismantling or Balso Snell's constant dreaming—but it is more terrifying: "When he fell asleep, he was always afraid that he would never get up." One part of Homer is not passive: his hands. They demand special attention (like Anderson's Wing Biddlebaum) because they contain the violent energy his body tries to suppress. They reassert themselves. Homer is a battlefield (remember the army metaphor!) with opposing forces. He must control the hands by various ritualistic activities—by plunging them into cold water; hiding them in a towel; and trying to forget them.

Homer is also described as a "poorly made automaton." He is puppetlike, answering the commands of some master; he tries all the while to spring to life. Is he object or spirit? The question catches his ambiguous condition and reminds us that it is not different from the duplicitous atmosphere of Hollywood. Are any of the characters we have met, including Tod Hackett, as real as the films they serve? Do they, in fact, exist outside the camera?

Homer cries (of course, like a "dog and/or Peter Doyle). He tries to forget the sexual incident in his past. Once he worked in a hotel and had to get some rent from Romola Martin, the occupant of 611. He was ordered by the manager to collect. (He was always a puppet.) In 611 he noticed the alcoholic and perfumed woman. He broke down—his "head bobbed stiffly on his neck like that of a toy Chinese dragon." (The simile deftly combines the automaton, the childlike, and the romantic.) He became passionate—his violent energy asserted itself. Then the phone rang. "It was all over." He left the room, only to search desperately for her later. He returned to his routine (like an automaton) and came to California to live!

Now Homer gets out of his tub. His emotions are described as a cresting wave that never reaches the top. The wave collapses to "run back like water down a drain, leaving, at the most, only the refuse of feeling." Nature is again seen as a wasteland; water and sewage are mixed (as they are in *Miss Lonelyhearts*) to rein-

force West's excremental vision. Homer walks outside
after he dresses. Perhaps he is to be seen as an actor in
a film directed by a hostile director—he acts out the
script (of which he knows little), going through the
motions.[10] His personality fades into his performance.
He goes into a market where the unreal, colored spot-
lights stun him further.

Homer returns to his house to eat and sleep. His days
pass. (We are still in the flashback.) He seems separated
from his actions like a sleepwalker. Objects continue
to dominate him. The lizard is described at length.
Although he watches its movements with amusement,
he does not understand that it resembles him. It too
shifts about uneasily; it too is close to refuse; it too sits
for hours. The lizard disturbs him. Homer sides with
the flies. But he does not interfere in the battle. (We
are back to the "army.") He cannot act freely; he must
react.

In the next chapter Homer meets Harry Greener. The
meeting is very amusing because of their contrasting
motions. Harry does various clownish tricks, juggling
his derby hat, bowing, and jerking his body. Homer
stares, "clucks," and laughs silently. They discuss the
price of polish. After a while, Harry decides to practice
a victim's laugh in order to complete the sale. But the
laugh gets out of hand; it somehow crosses the line into
self-pity and leaves him exhausted. In terms of the
imagery pattern he cannot separate himself from his
performance. He yields to it and loses his freedom of
choice. He becomes an automaton: he is likened to a
"mechanical toy that had been overwound." His body
becomes spastic.

Homer is startled. (Perhaps he sees himself in the
sick clown.) He gives him some wine. When he opens
the door to get the sample case of polish, he (and we)
see Faye Greener for the first time. She is not very
kind. She responds to Homer's news about her father
"without giving any sign that she heard or cared."
Finally she bursts into the room, ignoring Homer, and

screaming "Now what in Hell's the matter?" Her in-difference and anger change suddenly—she is contra-dictory and two-sided as the men we have encountered—and she says "Charmed" to Homer. The cliché is par-ticularly funny. Faye now acts like the child she is dressed as—she hopes Homer can help her. Even he is puzzled by her "odd mannerisms and artificial voice."

West elaborates on both. Her mannerisms consist of arching her body in an "almost formal way." She en-joys being scrutinized. But her gestures are divorced from any meaning. Curiously they echo those of Homer's hands or Harry's spastic movements. They are "freakish," not belonging to the total pattern.[11] This is probably West's point. Faye is the mechanical toy, wound up to perform clichés. Her speech pattern is dis-jointed—she moves from the childlike "With plenty of mayonnaise, huh?" to "I adore it" in the same response to "salmon salad."

The meal shared by Homer and Faye is funnier than the previous conversation. He does not know what to do; he bustles about, trying to get her admiration (or just a smile). His frantic movements are in vain. She eats furiously, not looking at him. Her gobbling is sym-bolically justified—she devours all the men in the novel to gain some perverse kind of nourishment.

The psychological pattern interests West. He shows us that Faye can never regard men as more than ob-jects for her own satisfaction because she is so ambiva-lent toward her father. She hates his laughter—she is serious in a frivolous way—but is afraid to express it except by singing. She promptly sings "Jeepers Creepers!" with suggestive movements of her "but-tocks." The performance—he laughing, she singing—appears rehearsed; it allows them to give off steam. It usually ends with victory. Harry laughs higher so that his laugh becomes a "machinelike" screech. (The me-chanical intrudes once more.) Faye listens helplessly; then she grabs him and brings "her fist down hard on his mouth." The performance is over and she has repeated her victory. But she must extend her campaign —like an advancing army, she must conquer more men.

Now she resumes her childlike behavior. She sobs; she eats gingersnaps; and she claims that she will kill herself if she cannot become a star. Her speech gets away from her; so do Homer's itching hands. Their personalities reside in their mechanized behavior. The contrast between self and performance (or action) is dramatically evoked when Harry returns to the kitchen as though nothing had happened. He does a shuffle, calls her "child," and uses an "exaggerated backwoods accent." Homer merely thinks that the accent is funny and keeps silent. He does, however, agree to buy the miracle polish.

After they leave—Harry does not even look back— Homer returns to his reverie. (It is as if his dreams occur within the larger dream of his daily routine.) He sits on his hands. He must control his sexual energy. (West mentions his fingers twining "like a tangle of thighs.") He defends himself with chastity which serves him like "the shell of a tortoise, as both spine and armor." (Both the animal and army images are used.) He is, unfortunately, more troubled than ever.

He continues to think of Faye. He tries to escape into sleep, but he has forgotten the secret. Sleep is no longer "automatic"—the mechanical image again!—but a black patch on the other side of the tunnel. It is separate. He tries to amuse himself when he is awake by singing. The only words he knows are: "Oh, say can you see,/By the dawn's early light. . . ." (Does West intend us to note the reference to sight? All of the characters, especially Tod as artist, have a failure of vision, not being able to separate the real from the unreal.) [12] His words are empty. He thinks of travel— Hawaii, Mexico. Then he cries. But his flight into self-pity also fails because as West tells us, "to those without hope, like Homer, whose anguish is basic and permanent, no good comes from crying."

In the next chapter we return to Tod as participant-observer. The contrast between him and Homer is effective. He at least attempts to do something! (Nevertheless, we still are irritated by West's decision to devote the last six chapters to Homer.)

Tod visits Harry Greener's apartment. He is, of course, less interested in the old man than in Faye. (The irony between the passive father and the active daughter—between sickness and lust—is powerfully rendered.) He finds her affections "charming." We remember her own use of the word "charmed," and realize that Tod is under a spell—that Hollywood magic!—which allows him to forget her "amateurish, ridiculous play" and accept her.

Their conversation—they cannot touch—circles about dreams. Can they separate themselves from dreams? Must they give themselves? Should they be critical? Their questions—really Tod's—reflect West's fascinations with the idea of critical detachment which occurs in all of the novels. Here he goes to the center, showing how important it is for artists to be critics separated from their creations and yet somehow involved in them—or, to use his favorite metaphor, how to be actor and audience.

Faye has some critical ability. She is able to "laugh at her dreams" as she goes about creating them. But she is "mechanical"—a faulty craftsman. Her "critical powers" unfortunately stop at the "mechanics," not at the sources of her dreams, so that she constantly returns to vagueness. She "writes" a screen play which is concrete in details. It is, of course, full of clichés—a Tarzan figure; a spoiled young girl; a big storm; a snake; a rescue. She cannot finish because she cannot think through the plot. She is involved in it as wish-fulfillment.

Tod can separate himself from her plot, exerting his critical powers. He understands the sources of her dreams (and cliché art). However, West does not let him go free! Tod cannot see himself as actor with Faye —the silliness of his courtship. He is completely involved without knowing it and he loses himself in her blood-and-salt-tasting lips. He dreams of raping her. Thus his suppressed violence resembles that of Homer and Faye herself (in the previous confrontation-performance with her father). He is also directed by unknown forces.

Faye tells one last story about a young chorus girl who gets a "big chance." It is more "realistic" than the previous plot she has told, but it is also a "familiar version," a cliché-ridden work. Tod responds by saying that he likes it. He probably does, because he judges the teller, not the tale itself.

West has emphasized the dialogue about critical detachment, participation, clichés, and mechanics in order to lead up to the last paragraph of this chapter. Tod is inspired to work on his painting, "The Burning of Los Angeles." His art springs from physical frustration as does Balso Snell's or even Miss Lonelyhearts'.

In the painting Faye is the naked girl in the left foreground being chased by an "army" of men and women. (Tod would like to be in that army.) One woman is about to throw a rock at her, but she has her eyes closed. Faye is locked in dreams (as her previous storytelling confirms). She is enjoying the release of wild flight like a game bird bursting from cover in "complete, unthinking panic." (Note the reappearance of the "lower life" image.) The contrast between rigidity and wildness is interesting because it suggests that Faye strains against being "held," passive, or "automatic." So does Tod without putting himself in the picture, except, perhaps, in Faye's gestures. The painting is described — its sources but not its effects are given. The rest of the novel traces these effects of suppressing dreams.

More grotesques block Tod's access to Faye. One of these is Earle Shoop — the last name is wonderfully silly, rhyming with loop — who is a theatrical cowboy. He usually stands in front of a store which sells Mexican saddles, spurs, boots. It is his dream palace; he longs for the totems inside. West describes his physical appearance at length to stress his rigid and flat qualities (which make him another automaton). Earle has a "two-dimensional face that a talented child might have drawn with a ruler and compass." [13] His reddish complexion completes "his resemblance to a mechanical drawing."

Although Tod regards him as a "dull fool," he goes along with Faye when she meets him, even paying the check. We have another triangle. It is as if West must constantly return to the competition between men for a woman. I don't want to exaggerate the unnatural aspects of this relationship, but it is obvious that the Oedipal ties of Miss Lonelyhearts and now Tod are strong. Of course, we do not know enough about the latter's history to explain his motivations—this mystery is, indeed, one of the novel's limitations—but they are nevertheless curious.

Tod laughs at Earle and the other cowboys. He says "Howdy, partner"; they do not realize that they are being kidded. They are comic because they are out of place. Instead of talking about nature, they discuss road agents, show business. Their brutality is less funny—it fits into the violent atmosphere of Hollywood.

Faye arrives. She and her admirers climb into her car. They go through their usual performances. Earle claims that he has no money. Tod agrees to pay. Faye is bitchy. They drive to Earle's place in the mountains.

West describes the glories of nature which are in sharp contrast to the city they have left behind. He gives us orange poppies, "vibrant pink air," before he turns suddenly to the violence. He makes us see that nature itself is deceptive and brutal: a jay flashes by "squawking with its tiny enemy on its tail like a ruby bullet." The birds burst the air into particles "like metal confetti." Then he introduces the Mexican who has six game cocks—killers of a sort.

The outing grows in violence. Earle catches some quail—he is poaching—and their feathers are said to be "weighed down" by drops of blood. He cuts their flesh

with a pair of shears. Faye is squeamish but she gradually
gets excited. (Sex and violence always go together.) The
fire builds as does her passion. She does a bump-and-
grind routine to the lyrics of "They're fightin' their duels
about Tony's wife. . . ." [14] When she and the Mexican
dance, they engage in a love-war. Earle tries to join in
the "festivities" by whooping it up—note another rhyme
with his last name. He is unsuccessful. His violence is,
ironically, out of step with theirs—a "glass wall" (the
recurring window) separates them. He finally hits the
Mexican.

Now the riot begins. Tod chases Faye like a hound,
hoping to pull her to the ground. (He is as much of an
animal as the others.) He tingles even though he does
not catch her. He relaxes enough to think again of his
painting of Los Angeles "burning at high noon." The
city will have a "gala" air; the "people who set it on fire
would be a holiday crowd." The painting is said to be a
series of "cartoons" [15]—as this novel is—and it will
stylize the typical madness of America.

Tod has even more interesting thoughts. He wants to
be judged as an artist, not a prophet, but he believes
that he will be able to foretell the future. His painting
attempts to capture the future civil war: "The
Angelenos would be first, but their comrades all over the
country would follow." What would West say about his
accuracy in 1970 after three assasinations, Watts, and
Kent State?

Tod is ambivalent. He is amused and satisfied by his
prophecy of doom. Perhaps he feels that he has seen the
worst. He cannot be shocked anymore. He is wrong. The
chapter ends with his discovery that Faye and the car
are gone. He can be hurt again.

The disappearance of Faye is underlined at the beginning of the next chapter as Harry mentions to Tod
that she went to the pictures (with Homer). The old
man continues to be automatic—he is likened to a
clock which must be allowed to run down—as he
plunges into the past. He remembers playing a Jew

comic. (Where would West be without such slurs?) He
is so involved with his deathbed. His face is a mask
(another of West's favorite images) which cannot express anything "either subtly or exactly." It is, we can
say, as stylized as the character itself.

Tod wonders about Harry's suffering. He tries to go
through the mask (or, better yet, the window). He decides that even an actor suffers as "keenly as anyone,
despite the theatricality of his groans and grimaces."
Tod has progressed! He sees himself in Harry (and all
performers), bridging the gap between themselves.

Thus West permits Tod to listen closely to Harry's
past. (He fades into the other's life.) [16] Harry continues
to recall his previous performances as a youth on the
way to fortune, as married man, as deceived husband.
The clichés mount, but we consider them in a new light.
They come from pain. They are more than mere self-
indulgence.

West breaks the spell of communion. Faye returns
to blab about Homer, who is a "dope" and "strictly
homecooking." Her curt, silly remarks interfere with
our last vision of Harry—he is likened to "eroded
ground"; nature as wasteland again—and we are forced
to dislike her even more as a result.

Tod returns the next afternoon. He learns that Harry
is dead. The death is very important in the novel. It
compels Tod and Faye to chart new directions of behavior. For the present he sees her as a "poor kid"
(dressed, however, in a black lace negligee that had
large holes in it). He forgets her murderous sexiness.

But she is changed only in terms of her financial
condition. She continues to act—this time she is self-
accused. Perhaps she is justified in her guilt. When she
arrived home, she turned to the wall mirror. (Her narcissism means that she had joined the mirror-image—
she is not separated, as is Tod, from the "other side" of
things.) She looked at her pimple, working on it. She
got sore when Harry didn't respond—her back was
turned to him—and finally ran over to the bed to find

that he was dead. Now as she tells her story—it is in sharp contrast to her previous ones—she rocks back and forth. She cries—her tears are almost genuine.

West breaks the spell again. He refuses to allow us simple pity. He shifts our feelings to make us uncomfortable. He introduces the bustling Mrs. Johnson, the landlady who starts going on about the proper kind of funeral. Tod dislikes her. We can understand why. She coldly asks about money, city burial. Her "formal" conversation not only undercuts the tears of Faye—it makes the starlet aware of her precarious condition.

Immediately she decides on a new career. She will work as a whore for Mrs. Jenning. Her tear-stained face is fixed; her hard smile has taken control. The change startles Tod. (That he is able to be startled means his salvation—at least for the present.) He wonders about her previous tears and guilt. The chapter ends with his separation from her (and her friend, the whorish Mary Dove).[17] He is outside the door, trying to talk to them. He is answered by "Go peddle your tripe." We (and Tod) have come a long way from the presence of death through self-accusation to commercialized sex. Only a mature writer like West could have moved us so subtly!

The funeral occurs in the next chapter. Tod is said to be "drunk" as a result of his wanting to have the courage to fight with Faye. He is in an "ugly stage." His transformation is significant because it is parallel to Harry's —both have passed some "boundary"—and it demonstrates another aspect of his personality. He is a more complex person, not merely the artist-observer we have known, but he still does not emerge fully.

Tod views the casket. Harry is dressed in a tuxedo; his features have been shaped, plucked, and shaved. He resembles the "interlocutor in a minstrel show." Thus the theatrical imagery is still with us—it seems as if death itself is a kind of performance for the spectators. Tod bows his head in prayer—perhaps he wants to join the corpse, to get to "the other side," if only to paint it accurately. But he is interrupted by Mrs. Johnson talk-

ing about the lack of bronze handles on the casket.
(The use of fake materials is repeated.)

Tod notices Faye and runs to her. She wears a "tight"
black dress and she has her platinum hair tucked up
under her hat. The incongruities of her appearance are
noted. They talk in a empty showroom which contains
photographs of tombstone and mausoleum. They kiss
for the first time. More incongruities! Tod pleads for
more—his ugliness is asserting itself!—and although
she rages at him, he admires her beauty, not her mind
or heart. She resists. He begins to offer an argument
about the diseases which can destroy her beauty. She
runs away.

Tod attempts to leave the chapel, but Mrs. Johnson
directs him to a seat for the services. (She reminds us
of the fat man directing the army at the beginning.) He
looks at the audience—at Faye, Mary Dove, Abe
Kusich—as he sits alone (significantly!) in the seventh
row. Then he notices the other spectators. They have
come not to mourn for Harry but to see, if possible, a
dramatic incident. They stare back at him with "an
expression of vicious, acrid boredom that trembled on
the edge of violence." They have come closer to him
since the opening chapter when he first mentioned them.
Soon they will be on top of him.

Tod takes his eyes away. He concentrates upon
people he has already met. The Gingo family are Eski-
mos who have settled in Hollywood after having made
a film about "polar exploration." They had shared
maatjes herrings they bought at Jewish delicatessens
with Harry. They are unlike Tod because they have
yielded to the surroundings and found a home. They
do not see the grotesque quality of their assimilation.

The overhead lights dim; other lights go on behind
"imitation stained-glass windows." (The description
combines the fakery and the glass patterns.) The music
starts. Tod remembers the Bach chorale, "Come Redeemer, Our Saviour," as the song which his mother
often played. (This is the first time that she has been
mentioned. We do not know the influence she had upon

his personality. In her "empty" quality she resembles Miss Lonelyhearts' mother.) He thinks of Christ in the music as a "maiden surrounded by maidens"—perhaps the feminine aspects of Miss Lonelyhearts come to mind—and he knows that the audience will respond only to Christ as a more powerful being. He is right—the Gingos grow "uneasy." But then the music changes again. The threat and impatience disappear; gentle love triumphs. Tod knows finally that Christ gives no sign to his audience. He remains separated by the music; he cannot redeem Hollywood.

The service ends. (Is there a pun or service? Neither Christ nor the spectators can serve each other.) The "friends" approach the coffin. They are unsure about the proper response. They cannot offer the usual re-action, the cliché. They are afraid and retreat. Tod uses the awkward situation to escape from the chapel. He does not realize that there is "no exit," no final separa-tion from the others.

After the funeral Tod returns to his work at the studio. He is, appropriately enough, at the window—his characteristic position!—when he sees Mrs. Jenning dressed in costume for *Waterloo*. He calls to her, but she does not wait. He runs after her. The detail is important because it shows his impatience and his need to participate. When we first saw him at the window, he did not go outside. Now he does. He is not the same.

Tod enters the world of dreams (or gets closer to the center of the entire Hollywood dream). He is a Balso Snell inside the horse. He moves through the fake ma-terials—an "ocean liner made of painted canvas"; a papier-mâché sphinx; a backless "Last Chance Saloon"; the skeleton of a Zeppelin—and he gets dusty, hot, on edge. He loses his breath because he cannot control the environment. He is merely part of some lunatic design. He is being dreamed! Tod finds that he is ordered—like the army at the beginning. Who is in charge of these commands? Surely not the Greek god lying "face downward in a pile of old newspapers and bottles!"

Tod tries to find a shape for his frantic wandering.

He thinks of such artists as Rosa, the painter "of Decay and Mystery." He was able to create art out of "armories of spikes, hooks, and swords"; of "partially demolished buildings." Tod wants to capture the "dream dump." He must give it a pattern and redeem it—Christ won't!—through art. He thus sees himself as the savior—another Miss Lonelyhearts. It is at this point that he becomes West's double. Both artists rage for order, taming the materials of the imagination.

Tod breaks his reverie. He arrives at the set of *Waterloo*. He smells the pungent odor of blank powder. (The powder may be as blank as the historical event the movie invokes.) He hears the fake noises of battle—canvas is torn to sound like children whimpering. He is aware of the deception, but he still must solve the problem of making true art out of unreal, junk-filled clichés. In any event he never does locate Mrs. Jenning.

Tod returns to the office in a studio car with several extras. They are happy over their wounds because they can get more wages. The juxtaposition is ironic. He has been an extra (an outsider), but he has received no compensation for his injuries. At the office he finds Faye, who claims that his previous lecture had converted her and "brought her to her senses." She is now living with Homer in a strictly business arrangement—her expenses are being paid for. He is happy that his lecture has succeeded.

Tod visits them. He learns that Homer (who has a flower in his buttonhole) does the housework, brings her breakfast in bed, and buys her clothing. He dislikes his "happy grin," believing that Faye has chosen him for his money. Tod is more defeated now than in the previous chapter.

His thoughts are broken by a woman's shouts. She screams "Adore! Adore!" The words—we learn later that she is calling her son—are appropriate after the conversation between the two men (both adore Faye). Maybelle Loomis keeps shouting as she informs them that she is trying to get Adore into films. She is an old settler, having lived in California, a "paradise on earth," for six years. She gives them more information. She is a vegetarian, following the commands of Dr. Pierce, her spiritual leader. (His ads say "Know-All Pierce-All." The slogan is carefully chosen to contrast with Tod's inability to know all and to "pierce" Faye or the mysteries of the dream-dump.) She says: "Death comes from eating dead things." Her simple-minded faith consists then of a series of clichés—she finds "romance" in religious slogans.

Adore appears. He is perhaps the most grotesque character in the novel. He has no personality (or appearance) except that given to him by Hollywood. He is filled by clichés. He is at home here, but to a relative outsider like Tod, he seems unreal and unbalanced. Adore is dressed like a man; his eyebrows are "plucked and shaped carefully"; his gestures are mechanical. He rages against his mother (and the world), but he can express his anger only in tantrums. He submits to his mother's "pleas" and sings a song: "Mama doan wan' *no peas.* . . ." (West uses the words to reinforce the law-giving aspects of Maybelle Loomis.) He makes suggestive gestures with his hands, he cries with "sexual pain." Adore does not know the sexual pain felt by Tod (and Homer); he is a masquerader.

Tod is happy to see him leave. (He does not want to be with a kind of grotesque double of himself.) He is excited by the reappearance of Faye (who looks "uncontaminated by thought") and somehow depressed at the same time because he cannot get through her "smooth surface." He runs from her and returns to his art.

Tod visits different Hollywood churches. His quest for "models" begins to resemble that of Miss Lonelyhearts. (For that matter all of West's heroes search. Their adventures inform the wandering structure of *The Dream Life of Balso Snell*, *A Cool Million*, and this novel. *Miss Lonelyhearts* alternates more swiftly between quest and retreat; it is a tighter work.) He is looking for salvation through religious art; he wants his painting to incarnate spiritual truth. Tod sees the dream palaces of holiness in which various objects or materials become totems (in much the same way Hollywood costumes falsely suggest transcendent values): in the "Church of Christ, Physical" chestweights are used to acquire holiness; in the "Tabernacle of the Third Coming" a woman in male clothing preaches against "salt."

Tod is beyond pity or satire. He thinks of the worshippers with "respect," knowing their furious power. When he stares at a midwesterner preaching a "crazy jumble of dietary rules, economics and Biblical threats," he responds to his "messianic rage." He realizes that the entire congregation (which sings "Onward Christian Soldiers") has the power to "destroy civilization." He fears the religious army (the metaphor returns) marching to victory. The chapter ends on this doom-filled, prophetic note.

The warfare grows in the next chapter (on a more private scale). We learn in the first paragraph that Faye is bored with Homer and the life they lead. She begins to persecute him—as she did her own father. Homer increases his servility. He resembles a "cringing, clumsy dog." (West reintroduces the animal imagery here, reminding us again of Peter Doyle in *Miss Lonelyhearts*.) They are close to a "final crisis."

Tod (who was not mentioned earlier in the chapter) is on hand to view their separation. He goes with them to the "Cinderella Bar," a building in the shape of a lady's slipper. It specializes in shows by female impersonators. (The fakery continues.) Faye, not satisfied with her prince(s), forces Homer to drink champagne, telling him that she (as "mama") will spank him. He drinks in a sloppy way. She then goes after Tod; she claims that even though she worked as a whore, she cannot yield to his advances. Meanwhile Homer gets outrageously drunk, grinning and coughing loudly.

Their performances—is Homer really happy? does

Tod accept Faye's refusal? is she vicious or sweet?—are linked to the performance on stage as a young man in a "tight evening gown of red silk" sings "*Little man you're crying. . . .*" The actor and spectators are no longer sure where they are. They have been transported by love (or illness). The young man is "really a woman" at one point; then he imitates a man as he strides off stage. Faye barks at Homer; she is more of a bitch than a woman.

Faye leaves to dance with Earle Shoop—this way she can torture all the men. Homer starts talking about a "dirty black hen" which is bloody and scabby. The bird owned by a Mexican Mig (who now lives in Homer's garage!) is a fighter in contests; it becomes a symbol of the martial, animalistic people who watch it.

In the next chapter Tod and Claude Estee drive to Homer's place for the cockfight. West describes the atmosphere in great detail, giving us laughter, headlights, and tension. Abe, one of the spectators, is "fidgety"; he shoves Tod, screams at Earle. Somehow they all laugh again, and everything is "fine." Mig takes his bird and shows it to the other men. The feathers are "tight and hard" and look as though they had been varnished. (West uses the metallic image again.) The body is "like a truncated wedge." This bird is pitted against another.

The fight is described at great length (perhaps as much as any scene until now). It is a ritualistic set piece in which time stops. The men lose their identities; they gaze intently at the birds, almost worshipping them. The fight is, then, a substitute for religion and art—it carries their dreams or aspirations.

Instead of bringing out the best qualities of the men, the fight encourages them to surrender to their need for violence and self-destruction. West gives us such sentences: "The red turned with the gaff still stuck in him and pecked twice at his opponent's head." These are cut through by the shouts of Earle: "Pit 'em." The climax is reached as one bird drives a "gaff through one of the red's eyes into its brain. The red fell over stone dead."

The chapter ends with the men respectfully handling the dead bird. Tod passes the whiskey. The cockfight is over, but the men will continue to fight. Faye is the prize. She is introduced at the beginning of the next chapter wearing a sexy outfit. She pats Abe on his head; she gives Tod her hand; she charms Claude; she orders Homer to bring more whiskey; she speaks to Earle and Mig with "stilted condescension." They all sit and drink, except for Faye. She stands so that the men can admire her body. She "peacocked for them all." (She is now a bird; previously she was a bitch.) She is courted by each man and she, in turn, courts Claude so that she can get a chance in pictures. Her performance —again we have the scene of actor and spectator—is skillful because she separates herself from her audience. In a strange way she resembles Tod in being able to "form" her models—the adoring men—for her "art." But like Tod she gets too involved with the design. She is caught in her dreams of glory.

The irony is that the spectators do not really hear her. They are too busy watching all of her gestures— her crossing and uncrossing her legs; her secret smile; her shivering—to consider her as a person. She is simply an object for them (and their dreams). Tod is different. He is drunk, but he is able to stand outside of the performance, noting the motives of Faye and the men. Nevertheless, he cannot take the tension. He leaves.

Tod is followed by Homer. The two of them share a secret alliance because they have been wounded in different ways by Faye. They are her unhappy, frustrated lovers. Tod tries to offer advice but retreats into silence. Homer flees to his complicated tic: his hands move back and forth, "struggling to get free." Suddenly they hear Faye's voice singing: *"Dreamed about a reefer five feet long. . . ."* It promises obscure delights.

Homer is shaken. He pleads with Tod (or "Toddie" as he childishly calls him) to help him get rid of Mig and the others. He is told that Faye is a whore; she isn't worth the trouble. Homer grunts. The final sound of the chapter is Faye's husky voice proclaiming *"Everything is dandy. . . ."*

Things become more complicated. Tod returns to the house. (Throughout the novel he leaves and returns!) He finds Faye and Mig dancing slowly for the spectators; he is too angry to be hypnotized. He tries to find Homer to express sympathy, but he is rejected. He is drawn back to the living room.

Passions have been let loose. Earle and Faye stumble and bump against the walls. They laugh. But Abe (now referred to more often as the dwarf) barks and lowers his head like a goat—he wants to dance with Faye. He is then likened to a "tiny ram" as he charges Earle's groin. (The combination of animal behavior, violence and sex is artfully rendered here.) The confusion mounts. Miguel throws Abe against the wall, like "a man killing a rabbit against a tree." Finally there is some peace when the dwarf loses consciousness.

Tod and Claude decide to leave. When they try to force Abe to go with them, he starts raging and calls them "punks." He wants more action, more girls. He tells them to go to hell after they refuse his request. It is fitting that the chapter ends with Abe driving away: "He let out the brake and the car rolled away." There has been no "brake" at Homer's house.

When Tod wakes the next morning with a headache and stays in bed until noon, we realize that he is suffering more than a simple "hangover." He cannot face future shocks (resembling Miss Lonelyhearts at the end of the novel). Somehow he manages to pull himself together and go to Homer. The house is different. No gamecocks; no cars; no noise—the silence is complete. He shouts hello, hoping to reach someone. Only Homer is there. He is even more paralyzed than Tod, neither moving nor answering any questions.

There is little communication. Homer shakes his head like a dog. He continues to sit in one place. Tod tries to give him some coffee, but he is ignored as the rejected "keeper" announces that he is returning to the Midwest. Now the first sounds break through the silence. Homer cries like an "ax chopping pine, a heavy hollow, chunking noise." (The use of the simile reminds us again of natural violence.) Once he starts, he cannot control himself. He speaks rapidly like a dam bursting: "The more he talked the greater the pressure grew because the flood was circular and ran back behind the dam again."

Tod cannot understand Homer's words until he notes that they are simultaneous, not continuous. (They are like the flashing images on a screen.) They almost rush past him, but he is able to stop the flow somewhat and learn that Faye moved out after calling Homer "all sorts of dirty things." She had been caught in bed with the Mexican, and had decided to leave the men.

Homer regresses further. He curls "into a ball," but he cannot relax. He is likened to a "steel spring" which tries to attain the shape of its "original coil." He wants to return to the womb—isn't this a desire to break through the window separating past from present, death from life?—and his "uterine flight" reminds Tod of a woman's picture in some psychology textbook.

Tod does not know what to do with Homer because he secretly desires to follow him. He thinks with longing of the womb as a "perfect escape"—better than the ones offered by religion or art. It is viewed as a hotel where the feeding is "automatic." (West continues, as in *Miss Lonelyhearts*, to associate food and women.) "The grave wasn't in it." Tod has descended a bit more since we first met him. He was able to keep his distance from the flow of grotesque humanity and to paint "objectively." After his drinking—a loss of distance— he permitted himself to get involved. He broke the window! Now he lets his unconscious needs control him. He paints less because art is less significant (and real) than his desire to escape his "destiny." The only problem is that West does not really indicate the reasons for (or sources of) Tod's sudden decline. He shatters the image we have had in an unexpected, inadequately prepared way.

Tod escapes from confronting the "perfect escape" by leaving Homer and going to the saddlery store. He forces himself to believe that he is there only to learn about Faye and Earle. He indulges in small talk (which reminds us of the racial slurs of *A Cool Million*) with "Chief Kiss-My-Towkus," a Yiddish-speaking Indian. He gets some information about Faye, and he speculates that she cannot be hurt. She will survive the waves (unlike Miss Lonelyhearts who surrendered to them): "He pictured her riding a tremendous sea. Wave after wave reared its ton on ton on solid water and crashed down only to have her spin gaily away." Tod considers her as a "cork"—an object without personality—defying the elements.

In a restaurant he continues his fantasy. (Again we have food and women!) He pictures raping her in the chill, spice-smelling dark. She is a "deer" unexpectedly caught by an oncoming truck. But he cannot pursue the fantasy. The waiter—is he supposed to resemble the "tyrannical" director of the first chapter or Mrs. Johnson at the funeral?—commands him to eat his steak. Tod loses the fantasy and leaves the restaurant.

The preceding scenes were short. Interruptions destroyed fantasy (Homer's and Tod's). Now in the final chapter West hits us with the long, apocalyptic fulfilment of fantasy; the various dreams become the final nightmare.

Tod reaches the street and sees "violent shafts of light" moving across the sky in "crazy sweeps." The emphasis is, as usual, upon the visual qualities of reality, but by means of such adjectives as "crazy," the "unreal" and "invisible" take over. (Does West mean to suggest "violent" with "violet"?) The shafts of lights are disturbing especially when they become "fiery columns." "Columns" reminds us of the army metaphor. Kahn's Persian Palace Theatre is lit; it is the scene of a world premiere—a new event in the dreams of men.

Tod is unsure about where he belongs. He begins to

walk to Homer's place, but he quickly changes his mind. He decides to kill time by looking at the crowds. (The cliché "kill time" becomes ominous as the hints of violence increase.) He is drawn to them, secretly identifying with their needs for violence (and rape). At the theater he enters a lane despite the commands of the policeman—he rebels here against the authorities—and joins the crowd. But he is afraid. He hears screams, catcalls, yells. His ability to visualize the crowd (as others) is lost as he listens to and touches it. It is suddenly a "dense mass"—an army to defeat any other force—which can "surge" forward when it desires. (It resembles the threatening "waves"; it is as natural as the sea.)

Some people stand out briefly. There is a young man whose hysterical voice whips the crowd into an ecstasy. He is likened to a "revivalist preacher"; his religion supplants the Christ of the Bach chorale. It appeals to the masses, promising as it does excitement and stupendous noise. The police tell him and his followers to move. West demonstrates that the crowd still lacks an objective and lets itself be shoved, "just as a bull elephant does when he allows a small boy to drive him with a light stick." (We have come far from the puppy—qualities of Homer or the lizard he watched. Now we have big animals.)

Tod returns to the scene. It is as if he had lost his consciousness in the crowd. However, he is no longer the person we knew. He whirls angrily; he squirms; he pushes. He manages through great effort to wrench free. He sits on the low retaining wall and tries once more to be an objective observer.

The visual is emphasized here as he separates himself. He sees "whole families" of dull, empty faces—many are old, bored, and disappointed—and he speculates about the reasons they have come to take the stage in one final performance. He imagines their having slaved at some kind of heavy labor and having saved pennies dreaming of paradise in California. They have grown tired of avocados and "passion fruit." (West puns on the latter, showing that they lack the real passion for experience and truth.) They have waited for some revelation, if only of doom, but it has not come to redeem their entrapped lives. Thus they wait here for the ultimate sign. The second coming will be at the movies!

Tod stands up from the wall (where, appropriately enough, he has had his cleansing vision) and intends to return to Homer's place. He does not need further visions in the crowd. Suddenly he sees the poor soul walking toward him and looking more than ever like "a badly made automaton"—his features are "rigid and mechanical." His appearance is even more grotesque because of his open fly (through which we notice a nightgown!) and his suitcases. Homer is unbalanced, not knowing where to turn; the suitcases are poor "balance weights."

Tod is almost separated from him as the crowd lurches—the physical separation is, of course, symbolic of his mental separation—but he sees Homer moving blindly in front of powerful cars. At last he reaches him. They sit quietly near each other fifty feet from the crowd.

The moment is set for violence. Tod observes a boy—it is Adore Loomis!—playing hide and seek with Homer. The boy darts from behind the eucalyptus tree, jerks a string attached to an old purse near the bench, and runs away. He repeats the action many times, hoping to lure Homer to open the purse. (The purse is like the Hollywood dream which tantalizes the crowd until it is discovered to be empty.) Tod tries to get him to stop, but Adore's nastiness—which was evident the first time we met him—is out of control. The boy throws a stone at Homer.

The violence grows. Homer springs alive (perhaps like the "original coil" mentioned previously?). He stamps on the boy with all of the power he had repressed. He is a "stone column." (The linkage of rigidity and martial violence is apparent.) Although

Tod desperately hits Homer, he cannot budge him because the midwesterner has finally directed his hands —or have the hands directed him?—toward someone weaker.

The crowd worships this ultimate sign. It charges like a mad army, shoving Homer "against the sky" and cresting over Tod. Tod is terrified as he is "carried backwards," returning to the unconscious drives he has tried to escape through his art. He is swept along, then "turned again and again, like a grain between mill-stones." (The stone image reasserts itself.) He rises into the air—a mock ascent!—although he fights to keep himself on the ground.

Tod finds himself in a "dead spot." He is able to turn his body only by twisting the body of a skinny boy pushing against him. His pain does not diminish. Then he faces a young girl with a torn dress. One of her thighs is between his legs. (His earlier dreams of raping Faye have ironically come to this!) He struggles to get free of her, but she cannot stop because an old man is biting her neck. The chain of violence is powerful. Tod grabs the man's ear and pulls hard—the movement liberates the girl. He has saved her.

There is no way out for Tod. He is swept along again —the waves overwhelm him as they did Miss Lonely-hearts—and he sees another man grab the girl with the torn dress. Although he finds himself in another dead spot with friendly people (shorter than he is), he realizes that they too have lost their senses. They are unable to distinguish between fact and fiction. They delight in calling others "perverts." (Homer is labeled as one for attacking Adore.) They joke about tools, pillows, and riots.

Their noise is lost in the siren blast of an ambulance. They start moving again, pushing Tod along, slamming him against the base of an iron rail near Kahn's Pleasure Palace. He holds on for dear life (even kicking a woman who tries to hang on to him or the rail). He "thinks clearly" of his painting, "The Burning of Los Angeles," and he can see all of it in his mind in a less "automatic" way.

The painting is the "still point" in this lengthy, rushing chapter. It gives shape to the frenzy Tod has just felt. It contains a great mixture of architectural styles—remember the many descriptions of phony houses (culminating in Kahn's Pleasure Palace?)—and the faces of all the cultists—"all those poor devils who can only be stirred by the promise of miracles and then only to violence." They march behind the banner of a super "Dr. Know-All Pierce-All," joyously worshipping the flames. They are the center of the painting (and this novel). In the lower foreground are Faye, Harry, Homer, Claude, and Tod caught in characteristic gestures: Faye holds her knees high in flight; Harry stumbles along; Homer sleepwalks, "his big hands clawing the air in anguished pantomime"; Claude thumbs his nose at his pursuers; and Tod throws a small stone.

Tod continues with the painting but he is startled by a policeman trying to push him into a group waiting for medical help. He does join his disheveled brothers. The ambulance siren—the trumpet of judgment day?— makes him laugh and he begins to imitate it "as loud as he could." The novel ends with this final masquerade.

The Day of the Locust is a novel of Hollywood. I stress the setting because it dominates the citizens. The most powerful scenes are, indeed, those in which it truly becomes the protagonist.

West is so concerned with Hollywood that he tends at times to forget the center of consciousness. Tod shifts before our eyes, changing his role as actor and spectator. We are troubled by these sudden losses of identity, but once we realize that he surrenders to Hollywood, we do not mind his absence. We understand that it is perfectly appropriate.

The fact that West wants to capture Hollywood suggests to us that he broadens his canvas. He gives us many sights, many corners, many angles. He roams—

more so than in *Miss Lonelyhearts*. This novel is, therefore, loose, wide, and free. But West is too much of a craftsman to let it get completely out of control. By employing such recurring images as animals (or insects), windows, sexual confusion, actor-spectator, he keeps the upper hand. *The Day of the Locust* is saved, finally, by its intense vision of Hollywood. We do not easily forget its violence and unreality. The day of the locust—not the weak characters—haunts our dreams.

6

Epilogue

The four novels vary is quality—the two most powerful ones are, of course, *Miss Lonelyhearts* and *The Day of the Locust*—but they share remarkable similarities of theme, character, and symbol. We would expect this kind of similarity because West is, like such other American writers as Poe, Hawthorne, Melville, and Faulkner, an obsessive artist. I underline the noun to indicate that he does not merely throw "narcissism," quest, etc. at us and force us to pattern them; he shapes his dreams in complex ways that demand the close readings I have given.

The novels resemble lyrics. They are constructed tightly—except for *A Cool Million*—because they stress image, not idea. This is not to imply that they do not deal with important themes—West writes about the most important ones we can consider: destiny, wisdom, "reality"!—but to suggest that they are, after all the analyses, symbolist designs. If we neglect the performer, the mirror, or the room, we misread (misunderstand) the meaning. Image is idea; form is content.

I find that although I have explicated the symbols—ideas of the novels (and, hopefully, such structural devices as the disappearing narrator or the dream-within-dream), I have not devoted much time to the style of individual paragraphs. Here I want to analyze some paragraphs to demonstrate how they embody West's total vision. (It is, finally, by paragraphs that we read novels; they are the building blocks which support complete structures.)

The choice of typical paragraphs is, of course, a difficult task. I do not want to choose them from *A Cool Million*—the writing is slack and cute. *The Dream Life of Balso Snell* offers many good choices—I am thinking especially of the body as army—but they are "unrepresentative." There is much poor writing in this first novel. The paragraphs should come from *Miss Lonelyhearts* or *The Day of the Locust* because these novels are the ones which will endure; they are, indeed, the reasons any critic studies West.

My paragraphs come from *Miss Lonelyhearts*:

> Miss Lonelyhearts found himself developing an almost insane sensitiveness to order. Everything had to form a pattern: the shoes under the bed, the ties, in the holder, the pencils on the table. When he looked out of a window, he composed the skyline by balancing one building against another. If a bird flew across this arrangement, he closed his eyes angrily until it was gone.
>
> For a little while, he seemed to hold his own but one day he found himself with his back to the wall. On that day all the inanimate things over which he had tried to obtain control took the field against him. When he touched something, it spilled or rolled to the floor. The collar buttons disappeared under the bed, the point of the pencil broke, the handle of the razor fell off, the window shade refused to stay down. He fought back, but with too much violence, and was decisively defeated by the spring of the alarm clock.

The paragraph opens quietly as Miss Lonelyhearts finds himself acting in a strange way. The first sentence is matter of fact, passive ("found himself"), and "qualified" ("an almost insane sensitiveness"), but it deals with growing insanity. There is great tension between the arrangement of words and their meaning. What is happening? How can West (and Miss Lonelyhearts) be so calm? Such questions are deliberately suggested by the sentence. There is, of course, an emphasis upon "order." Miss Lonelyhearts must find correct patterns. The first (and each preceding) sentence apparently affirms his ordered arrangement.

West moves from the general ("order," "everything") to the specific. His sentence alerts us to detailed experience; thus he introduces such objects as "shoes," "ties," and "pencils"; these must go along with "bed," "holder," and "table." The sentence itself puts specifics in order; the colon lines up the following, listed objects. Everything seems neat.

But the paragraph turns again. In the third sentence Miss Lonelyhearts tries to extend his vision—note the emphasis on visual experience!—by moving from specific objects in his room (his sanctuary, his closed consciousness) to the external skyline. He balances internal and external things; he "composes" to gain composure; he stares at and performs in reality. (West puns on "composed" in a characteristic way to suggest tense ambivalence.) The third sentence is also tight.

But the fourth sentence is out of place and destructive. The bird (another living thing) blots out the arrangement; its actions are described first and, therefore, are more prominent than those of Miss Lonelyhearts. He closes his eyes angrily. The adverb is the first one in the paragraph. (The emphasis has been upon adjectives and verbs—upon quantity or quality and action.) Its appearance suggests that action is now being measured; how Miss Lonelyhearts reacts is as significant (especially later in the novel) as the nature of things surrounding him. The sentence (and the paragraph) ends with "gone." This last word suggests that change has occurred—the pattern has been defeated. One detail is oddly victorious.

The second paragraph begins with reversal. Miss Lonelyhearts seems—to use another characteristic word—to be back in control. His control is, unfortunately, only "for a little while." The phrase is interesting because it alerts us to time as an element of consciousness. Miss Lonelyhearts—like all of West's heroes—is barely aware of time except in relation to his obsession. Time, we can say, is obsessively measured; its presence is felt only when the ordered arrangement is in danger. "For a little while"—how little? How many days? We do not know because Miss Lonelyhearts does not know. The same is true of "one day" when he "found himself with his back to the wall." The day is made specific in terms of defeat. The first sentence of reversal is in itself a reversal—triumph and defeat are mixed. Both are outside of Miss Lonelyhearts, who passively finds himself doing things correctly (or incorrectly). His "own" does not belong to him.

The second sentence repeats the day ("that day") during which all the inanimate things take the field against him. West intentionally uses the generalized description ("all the inanimate things") to suggest the terrifying, complete struggle against Miss Lonelyhearts. By stressing "inanimate," he makes us realize the insanity of his hero (who is himself compulsive, automatic, and "dead"). The word *things* turns into *something* in the next sentence—again the general is made specific. The verbs *spilled* and *rolled* wonderfully activate the situation; the combination of these two is mysterious. We are not immediately told what things are acting "erratically." There is suspense.

The fourth sentence clears up the matter in a detailed way. The details are the point after all; they are the things which disturb Miss Lonelyheart's pattern as they contribute to West's artistic pattern. There is a kind of mirror effect—West needs the details to build his structure; his hero, on the other hand, cannot tolerate details which destroy his arrangement. Can we say that West's style fights Miss Lonelyhearts' (showing us that it is necessary to accept and employ the details of experience)? In any event we get the "collar buttons," the "point of the pencil," "the razor," and "the window shade." These details are deliberately small (or "insignificant") to underline the impatient madness of Miss Lonelyhearts.

The fourth sentence is the longest in the paragraph because West gives all power to the things. Furthermore, he makes their actions ("disappeared," "broke," "fell off," and "refused to stay down") apply symbolically to his hero who "disappears" in the sentence and thus proclaims his defeat. Should we make much of the shape of these objects? Most can be seen in Freudian terms ("round," "point"). If they were dreamed, they could be interpreted in various sexual terms. Perhaps Miss Lonelyhearts is afraid of them because they symbolize male and female genitals. And what of the metaphysical design? The objects are more than sexual; they constitute reality—that reality which lies outside of his consciousness (or his "window"). They refuse to stay outside; they invade him.

The last sentence begins with Miss Lonelyhearts fighting back—all of West's heroes are on the defensive —but the combat is unsuccessful because he does not know how to measure things. What irony! He is so concerned with proper order that he is disordered. (Or vice versa.) He employs too much violence. His defeat is "decisive"—the finality is evident when West introduces the "spring of the alarm clock."

So the two paragraphs are complete. Although they begin with Miss Lonelyhearts "developing," they end with the ultimate victory of the clock. He is defeated by time—he cannot remain a child or innocent. There is no hope for his redemption. Everything—the rage for order, extreme violence, madness, the hostility of nature —has been rendered in a deceptively simple, tight arrangement. Miss Lonelyhearts, we can say, is defeated by West's stylistic finality.

But there is one more point. We are given some hope because we recognize that no matter how much we may hate art, calling it false or inhuman as Balso Snell did, we are pleased that it can illuminate the inadequacy of our designs. We are comforted by art—if it cannot rescue us from life's painful details, it can, nevertheless, alert us to them and by doing so, help us to scrutinize ourselves squarely and ironically. For this pleasurable, terrifying insight we are grateful to West's best novels.

Notes

1 — Approaches to the Novels

1. Cf. Randall Reid, *The Fiction of Nathanael West: No Redeemer, No Promised Land* (Chicago: University of Chicago Press, 1967), pp. 50–60 for a valuable study of the borrowings from Dostoevsky in *Miss Lonelyhearts*. Mr. Reid never relates West to such classic American writers as Poe, Hawthorne, and Henry James. I hint at this connection later in the chapter.

2. James F. Light, *Nathanael West: An Interpretative Study* (Evanston, Ill.: Northwestern University Press, 1961), p. 136. Light could have noted that rebellion against one's heritage partially explains the fiction of Hawthorne, Twain, and Faulkner.

3. Ibid, p. 138. Light does not pursue the great differences between these writers. Certainly Salinger's acceptance (?) of Zen should be contrasted to West's faithlessness and Bellow's hard-earned humanism.

4. Max F. Schulz, *Radical Sophistication: Studies in Contemporary Jewish-American Novelists* (Athens: Ohio University Press, 1969), p. 36.

5. Cf. my *Jews and Americans* (Carbondale: Southern Illinois University Press, 1965) for an exploration of traditional themes and literary devices in the work of Bellow, Malamud, Philip Roth, Isaac Rosenfeld, Karl Shapiro, Delmore Schwartz, and Leslie Fiedler.

6. Victor Comerchero, *Nathanael West: The Ironic Prophet* (Syracuse: Syracuse University Press, 1964) p. 163.

7. Cf. Stanley Edgar Hyman, *Nathanael West* (Minneapolis: University of Minnesota Press, 1962), pp. 22–24 for a controversial reading of *Miss Lonelyhearts* as a "homo-

sexual novel." Hyman tries to write the "hero's case history before the novel begins"; he offers no real justification for his description of the classic Oedipus complex. His reading, nevertheless, challenges all later critics of West.

8. Comerchero, *Nathanael West: The Ironic Prophet*, p. 3. Even in this paragraph he insists that West "reminds us that our behavior is rooted in sexuality." Cf. the definitive biography by Jay Martin, *Nathanael West: The Art of His Life* (New York: Farrar, Straus and Giroux, 1970) et passim for interesting biographical details about West's sexual attitudes and problems. I stress that these details never completely help us to read the final texts.

9. Reid, *Fiction of Nathanael West*, p. 77.

10. Nathanael West, "Some Notes on Miss Lonelyhearts," *Contempo* 3, May 15, 1933, 2.

11. Cf. David Bakan, *Sigmund Freud and the Jewish Mystical Tradition* (Princeton: D. Van Nostrand Company, 1958), for an intriguing analysis of the relationship between psychoanalysis and *kabbala*. He makes the point that Freud introduced such Jewish devices as secret wordplay and dream-interpretation into psychoanalysis.

12. Cf. Richard Chase, *The American Novel and its Tradition* (New York: Doubleday & Co., Anchor Books, 1957), p. 2, for this representative statement: "Oddity, distortion of personality, dislocations of normal life, recklessness of behavior, malignancy of motive—these the English novel has included. Yet the profound poetry of disorder we find in the American novel is missing, with rare exceptions, from the English." West surely gives us the "poetry of disorder."

13. John Hawkes, "Flannery O'Connor's Devil," *Sewanee Review* 70 (Summer 1962), 395–407.

14. Cf. my *New American Gothic* (Carbondale: Southern Illinois University Press, 1962) for a complete discussion of Capote, Salinger, Carson McCullers, Purdy, Hawkes, and Flannery O'Connor.

15. Hawkes, "Flannery O'Connor's Devil," p. 406.

2—The Dream Life of Balso Snell

1. West uses puns in all of his novels to suggest the two-faced quality of life. Holes, holy, Hollywood—the same kind of pun recurs.

2. It would be easy (and probably wrong) to see the authority figures as necessarily paternal, but there is no doubt

that they pose danger to the innocent hero. They are somewhat like the "reality-instructors" used by Bellow.

3. My interpretation of the anti-Jewish sentiments in the novel goes against the prevailing view that they are completely gratuitous. I am trying to show their relation to such recurring symbols as the circle.

4. West is obviously fascinated by food. In *Miss Lonelyhearts* and *The Day of the Locust* he associates food with women; lovemaking becomes "cannibalistic." Perhaps John Hawkes was inspired by West to develop the metaphor in *The Cannibal.*

5. Although West may mock Gilson and his "Russian" art, he is very indebted to the idea of the "underground man" in all of his novels. He even employs the metaphor in terms of burial and drowning. Cf. James F. Light, *Nathanael West: An Interpretative Study* (Evanston, Ill.: Northwestern University Press, 1961), p. 45, for a reference to Gilson as Raskolnikov. The echoes of Dostoevsky are also mentioned by Stanley Edgar Hyman, *Nathanael West* (Minneapolis: University of Minnesota Press, 1962), p. 14, and Randall Reid, *The Fiction of Nathanael West: No Redeemer, No Promised Land* (Chicago: University of Chicago Press, 1967), p. 23.

6. West often uses birds as symbols. Their meaning varies from the Inornata mentioned here (as vanity) to the shrike of *Miss Lonelyhearts* or the gamecocks of *The Day of the Locust.*

7. This circular movement reminds contemporary readers of Borges and his use of the maze.

8. The attraction and repulsion between performer and audience is curiously sexual. These tensions recur in all of the novels. It would be easy and misleading to locate their sources in West's ambivalent relationship to his first audience, his parents.

9. In *The Day of the Locust* West tries to redeem the cliché *"charming"* by concentrating upon the magic (or spell) it once conveyed. Even this first novel depends upon "hidden charms" which Balso pursues.

10. No critic, as far as I can tell, mentions Gogol as a possible source for the nose. I mention the Russian writer because his sense of irony (mixed with the sympathetic and grotesque) is close to West's. I do not want to belabor the comparison.

11. West uses water here in a parodic ritual of baptism.

In *Miss Lonelyhearts* and *The Day of the Locust* water is threatening, dirty, or "dead."

12. I underline this passage because it is the governing structure of the novel. Balso Snell cannot get out of his closed consciousness; he shuns marriage of any sort. No wonder that he (or West) appreciates mirrors! This novel, like the later ones, gives us the world as a reflection of the ill-formed self. Clearly such works as *Reflections in a Golden Eye, Wise Blood,* and *Malcolm* belong in the same tradition.

13. Salinger is another writer who makes much of the relationship of Christ and "performance." Zooey Glass teaches Franny to be a "religious actress"—to act for the Fat Lady. The same kind of attraction and repulsion, despite the easy message, exists toward the Fat Lady.

14. This two-faced O is another of West's powerful puns.

15. West continually uses sermons in his novels. They reinforce spiritual quality by stopping the flow of time. They are, as it were, "still points." Often, as in this context, they are also psychologically relevant to the preacher *and* audience.

16, This is still another face of O.

17. This novel ends with an army; so do A *Cool Million* and *The Day of the Locust.* The fact that the metaphor recurs should make us realize that it is beyond "politics." West is concerned with the "body politic."

18. West demands the purity of words. He wants to redeem clichés. In certain respects he resembles such writers as Beckett, Cage, and, of course, Salinger in trying to write about the glories of silence. Some critics would see the rebellion against "dirty words" as childishly narcissistic—the "sound of one hand clapping" is not easily heard by human beings.

3—Miss Lonelyhearts

1. In his "Some Notes on Miss Lonelyhearts," *Contempo* 3, May 15, 1933, 1, West writes that he wanted the novel to be " 'in the form of a comic strip.' The chapters to be squares in which many things happen through one action. The speeches contained in the conventional balloons." He tells us that he abandoned the idea but kept the notion of chapters as pictures. We can also relate the "tight frame" to the devices of his first novel. Both novels attempt to stop

time to fix it—actions, speeches, and thoughts seem frozen (thus peculiarly fitting for rigid thinkers like Balso Snell and Miss Lonelyhearts). Cf. Randall Reid, *The Fiction of Nathanael West: No Redeemer, No Promised Land* (Chicago: University of Chicago Press, 1967), pp. 84–91, for an interesting discussion of the "comic strip novel."

2. Many critics note the pun on "shrike," but they neglect the one on "pray." Nor do they make much of the other puns in the novel.

3. West uses italics in a suggestive way. They stand out from the rest of the page (as, indeed, the letters stand out in Miss Lonelyhearts' adventures). Is it reckless to imply that these italicized passages are indebted to his fascination with art (and even the balloon-captions of comic strips)?

4. It is wrong to stress the feminine qualities at the expense of religious suffering. Religion and sex marry in the novel.

5. Cf. Robert Andreach, "Nathanael West's *Miss Lonelyhearts*: Between the Dead Pan and the Unborn Christ," *Modern Fiction Studies* 13 (Summer 1966), 251–60 for valuable comments about the pun on "pan."

6. Cf. Edmond L. Volpe, "The Waste Land of Nathanael West," *Renascence* 13 (Winter 1961), 69–77.

7. West makes much of the word *pierce*. In *The Day of the Locust*, as we shall see, he uses "Dr. Pierce-All" as a kind of divinity. His fondness for puns may even extend to pierce-appears.

8. Stones are linked to Tod Hackett in *The Day of the Locust*. The latter pictures himself throwing a stone at the mob. Perhaps Lemuel Pitkin's name in *A Cool Million* belongs here, although he is more stoned (by the audience).

9. West returns often to man as machine. His "mechanized" metaphors remind us of the mechanician in Melville ("The Bell Tower") and to the many "automatons" in new American Gothic.

10. Although Reid, *Fiction of Nathanael West*, pp. 50–60, mentions *Crime and Punishment* as a source, he does not cite *The Brothers Karamazov* (which, of course, West does in the text). We think once more of Salinger and his use of the *Russian* pilgrim in *Franny and Zooey*.

11. I hope that I avoid the easy reductionism of religious needs to sexual ones. The coloring is very important.

12. Like the heroes of Poe, Hawthorne, Melville, and

Henry James, Miss Lonelyhearts is rigid ("stone-like," "automatic," "mechanical"). He regards the world as an object he must save because he identifies with it. External reality mirrors his consciousness. Miss Lonelyhearts has American as well as Russian ancestors.

13. Faye Greener in *The Day of the Locust* has "sword-like" legs. The sexual confusion should not be surprising—West has already given us a girl-man in *Balso Snell*.

14. Throughout the novel West gives us blasphemous or inverted symbols. Sanctuaries become nightclubs; divinities write for newspapers; baptism is dirty water. The list is endless.

15. I have noted West's obsessive use of "destructive" water. Cf. ch. 2, n. 11.

16. West uses "column" as army column in *The Day of the Locust*. The word carries three meanings.

71. The police recur as villians in *A Cool Million*. The sexual confusion in this passage is striking.

18. The marriage of people and objects occurs in new American Gothic and in the absurdist dramas of Beckett and Ionesco. West would feel at home in *The Chairs*.

19. Cf. Reid, *Fiction of Nathanael West*, pp. 91–97, for an interesting discussion of "ritual theater" in *Miss Lonelyhearts*.

20. The retreat into silence is, of course, an attempt to purge language of impurities in the most drastic, violent manner possible. It is suicidal.

21. The metallic and the martial metaphors will be developed at great length in *The Day of the Locust*.

22. West is already thinking of Hollywood and dreamlike violence. The *Blonde Beauty* title is wonderfully suggestive in this novel, connotating as it does great light.

23. The hands (and other distinguishing features) of Peter Doyle will appear again in the description of Homer Simpson in *The Day of the Locust*.

24. I do not want to emphasize the phallic quality here and to relate it to the final shooting, but I think that it should be mentioned.

4—A Cool Million

1. Randall Reid, *The Fiction of Nathanael West: No Redeemer, No Promised Land* (Chicago: University of

Chicago Press, 1967), p. 106, says: "Perhaps the first thing to be said about *A Cool Million* is that it is not very good." He is not alone in this opinion.

2. Cf. Jay Martin, *Nathanael West: The Art of His Life* (New York: Farrar, Straus and Giroux, 1970), et passim for biographical details about the commercial Jews known by West.

3. Mr. Whipple, like all of West's characters, is looking for a sign, an annunciation of truth. His patriotism is as religious in nature as Miss Lonelyhearts' search for holiness, but not as artistically rendered (largely as a result of West's basic need to go beyond politics).

4. The problem with these scenes is that we know that Lem will survive. Only at the end of the novel, when the physical dismantling is more vicious, do we acknowledge the fact of death. Even then we do not mourn for him—he remains an empty shell, not a "hero."

5. The "cold showers" echoes the advice given in *The Dream Life of Balso Snell*. West obviously finds the cliché very amusing.

6. West develops the "costume" metaphor in a different, more subtle way in *The Day of the Locust*.

7. It is unfortunate that West does not do more with politics as religion. The novel suffers as a result. There is a martyrdom and a resurrection—as well as a quest in the wilderness—but these are not developed completely as inverted or twisted ceremonies.

8. West returns to one guiding metaphor of all his novels. He is obsessed with role-playing because he sees it leading to several basic metaphysical questions: Is there a director? Can men create their own roles? In this novel he settles for an easier form of the question: Can men play their assigned roles in our social system?

9. No critics, as far as I know, probe West's ambivalence toward fascism. It reminds me of Mailer's in *Barbary Shore*.

10. The rape scene is obligatory in a West novel.

11. Surely this quotation demonstrates the contemporary flavor found even in West's poorest novel.

5—The Day of the Locust

1. Tod is, perhaps, more tortured than West's other heroes because he cannot control his roles as actor and

audience (performer and artist-spectator). He constantly shifts ground in the novel unlike Miss Lonelyhearts, who chooses (or is chosen) to remain in one role at the end.

2. Physical description is again limited. We see less of Tod than of the houses, movie sets, and freaks surrounding him.

3. West is closer to Gogol here than to such contemporary writers as Hawkes, Purdy, and Flannery O'Connor. But he is more ambivalent than Tod's statements imply. In the rest of the novel we detect a special rage allied with the grotesque—this rage interferes with complete sympathy for the "truly monstrous."

4. Houses reflect their owners. When the owners have no strong personality (sense of self) they adopt mixed, usual styles. West devotes much space to the psychology of architecture—from the narcissistic horse of Balso (his closed consciousness) to the iron-black room of Miss Lonelyhearts to the cathouse of Mrs. Jenning.

5. Cf. Randall Reid, *The Fiction of Nathanael West: No Redeemer, No Promised Land* (Chicago: University of Chicago Press, 1967), pp. 130–39, for a valuable discussion of the sources of the bitch-figure in *The Day of the Locust*.

6. The fact that she discusses Gertrude Stein is interesting. Miss Stein symbolizes two things: the confusion of sexual identity and the attempt to purify words. Both are important for West's novel(s).

7. We remember the deliberate (?) tedium of episodes in *The Dream Life of Balso Snell* and the descent into clichés in *A Cool Million*. At times West gives us "imitative form." In the blue movie scene he knows what he is doing; he wants us to enter the picture and share the frustration— he wants us to be more than spectators.

8. Cf. Reid, *Fiction of Nathanael West*, pp. 139–49, for an analysis of West's indebtedness to Anderson.

9. Cf. Jay Martin, *Nathanael West: The Art of His Life* (New York: Farrar, Straus and Giroux, 1970), p. 318, for the probable biblical sources of the novel's apocalyptic title. He suggests two sources: Exodus 10:3–6, 13–15 (the locust plague in Egypt) and Revelations 9:3–9 (the end of days: "And out of the smoke there came forth locusts upon the earth"). He also notes two possible contemporary sources.

10. Again we have the sense of restricted actions for West's characters. They seem to be moved by hostile out-

side forces (the metaphysical design) as well as hostile internal ones (the compulsive design). They surrender to determinism.

11. The characters in all of West's novels mirror one another. Despite the crowded canvas, there is really only one self seen in a series of cracked mirrors.

12. West's novel(s) strains toward an epiphany in which everything is seen purely. Such a vision is, of course, related to the attempt to create perfect words. Transcendence is the goal for both.

13. This quotation gets at the distinguishing features of West's novels. With great skill he gives us two-dimensional flat characters (or caricatures) who act in childish and rigid ways. He does not believe that human beings are well-rounded.

14. Throughout the novel, songs are carefully chosen to symbolize the feelings of the characters. Faye, for example, is "Tony's wife."

15. West drew cartoons. Martin, *Nathanael West*, reprints one of these (dated 1920). It pictures a sweaty anxious "performer" being photographed by two movie cameramen. At the age of seventeen West was already concerned with performer and audience, anxiety, and cartoon-exaggeration!

16. I have stressed the word *fade* many times. Perhaps West used the fade out as well as the "flashback" in this novel of film. The devices are psychologically valid.

17. Mary Dove as the name of a whore is brilliantly chosen. The slightest detail adds to the complex pattern!

Index

Abruptness, 34
Abstraction, 29, 47, 49
Activity, 31, 35
Aesthetic authority, 8
Allegory, 83
Ambivalence: tense, 121; West's, 131n9
Ambivalent, 25, 37
American Gothic, 8, 10, 130n18
Anality, 19
Anderson, Sherwood, 93
Andreach, Robert, 129n5
Animal behavior, 111
Anxiety, 12
Art: creates sickness, 16–17; and sadism, 17; claustrophobia of, 20; as reason for sex, 27; concern with, 31; sermon on, 34; value of, 42; in general, 50; as an escape, 52; mentioned, 10, 12, 14, 19, 29, 74, 87, 106, 107, 109, 112, 116, 123
Aspirations: heavenly, 3; mentioned, 109
Atheist, 8
Attraction: pattern of, 21
Austen, Jane, 7
Axiom, novelistic, 5
Axioms, narcissistic, 8

Bach, 52, 104
Bakan, David, 126n11
Barbary Shore, 131n9
Beauty, 17
Beckett, 128n18, 130n18
Beethoven, 52
Behavior: clownlike, 11
Bellow: linked with West, 2; mentioned, 125n3, 125n5, 127n2
Black comedy, 83
Blonde Beauty, 55
Body: concern with the, 14–15; mentioned, 17, 18, 29
Boone, Daniel, 77
Brahms, 52
Brothers Karamazov, The, 129n10

Cage, 128n18
Capitalism, 67
Capote, 9, 126n14
Carnegie Hall, 21
Castration, 3, 5
Chairs, The, 130n18
Character, 119
Characterization: and theme, 2; Jewish, 3
Chase, Richard, 7, 126n12
Christ, 25, 26, 27, 29, 34, 36, 38, 41, 42, 43, 49, 50, 52, 53, 58, 59–60, 63, 64–65, 74, 105, 106, 114

	DATE DUE	